AF378218

LITTLE BIT SILVERWARE

First published in 2014

A catalogue record for this book is available from the British Library

ISBN: 978-0-85733-729-0

Published by Haynes Publishing, Sparkford, Yeovil,
Somerset BA22 7JJ, UK
Tel: 01963 442030 Fax: 01963 440001
Int. tel: +44 1963 442030 Int. fax: +44 1963 440001
E-mail: sales@haynes.co.uk
Website: www.haynes.co.uk

Haynes North America Inc., 861 Lawrence Drive, Newbury Park, California 91320, USA

Images © Mirrorpix

Creative Director: Kevin Gardner
Designed for Haynes by BrainWave

Printed and bound in the US

LITTLE BIT
SILVERWARE

@wengerknowsbest

Foreword

John Cross, *Daily Mirror*

FOR a few of us regular Wenger watchers, this book will cause more than a "little bit" amusement.

In fact, Wenger Knows Best has been essential reading on Twitter for some time now as it captures the great man just perfectly.

And, put together, this book is an absolute must-read for any Arsenal fan and anyone who admires Arsène Wenger. It's all here and is a read which will have you smiling the whole way through.

His sayings, mannerisms, quirks and nuances are all here with a lovely mix of affection, humour and amusement.

Wenger Knows Best just captures him brilliantly – you can almost hear Arsène Wenger saying it as you read one of his quirky remarks.

What first got me hooked onto "Wenger speak" was a few years back when he uttered the word "footballistically".

Er, what, Arsène? I'm still struggling to figure out exactly what it means. Maybe, Wenger means in football terms... At least that's my take on it.

As the years have gone by, the affection has grown throughout the football world for one of the greatest managers of all time.

And this is not in any way poking fun at Arsène Wenger. After all – as I keep being reminded – not many managers can boast speaking as many languages as him.

French, German, Italian, Spanish, a bit of Japanese, and he'll have a bash at a few others if you ask nicely. When foreign journalists turn up at one of his press conferences, he'll always try to politely answer in whatever language the question is asked.

But, most of all, he speaks fluent Wenger. There are some common phrases in there. Like a "little bit", handbrake, I must tell you and super quality.

And if all else fails, Wenger will even have a crack at the hokey kokey. As he says in this book: "Ramsey in, Arteta out. In out in out, shake it all about. Suarez has said sorry and you turn around. That's what it's all about."

There's also Wenger code. The flat denial of the transfer is just about believable, a "little bit" wriggle room and the classic "he is an interesting player."

Wenger always keeps us amused with his sayings and catch phrases, and the magic of this book is that they are captured perfectly.

I'm not sure whether Arsène knows about Wenger Knows Best. I hope he'd find it amusing if he does. Because it's all meant in very good humour.

I salute the author. A few of us clocked him on Twitter and wondered whether he was an undercover journalist because he seemed to get every saying as if he was there every week. Not so.

To be this clever and perceptive, you must be something of an obsessive. Wenger is definitely an obsessive and so perhaps the Arsenal manager and his alter ego are perfectly suited for each other.

John Cross

Another Foreword

Arsène Wenger*

I don't know this book.

*Okay, not actually Arsène Wenger.

"I must say, I believe there is still a small small chance to sign Suarez..."
"I think so, I think so."
"But if not, we might go back in for Higuain, I don't know..."
"He has qua-lity..."
"Well yes. Look, it's good chatting with you as always. Are you close on any strikers for Napoli?"
"We must fo-cus..."
"Bendtner is looking sharp."

August 2013

Wenger Knows Best
@wengerknowsbest

There is still a month to go in the transfer market. Apart from all the teams that have made signings, nobody has done anything yet.

04/08/2013

August 2013

Wenger Knows Best @wengerknowsbest — Aug 1
We are delighted to confirm the signing of Edward Snowden on a free transfer from Moscow Airport.

Wenger Knows Best @wengerknowsbest — Aug 2
We like the Emirates Cup, we are up for it. Gazidis is being little bit coy, but he assures me Higuain was signed in time for his debut.

Wenger Knows Best @wengerknowsbest — Aug 3
Arsenal 2 Napoli 2 I must say, Napoli were strong opposition and started well, but maybe dropped little bit physically in the second half.

Wenger Knows Best @wengerknowsbest — Aug 3
I believe there is still a small small chance we can win the Emirates Cup.

Wenger Knows Best @wengerknowsbest — Aug 4
On the evidence of the Napoli match, did I make little bit mistake not signing Higuain? Yes you're right, Giroud did score a goal of exceptional quality.

Wenger Knows Best @wengerknowsbest — Aug 4
Chim-chiminee chim-chiminee chim chim chiroooo, who needs Higuain when we've got Giroud?

Wenger Knows Best @wengerknowsbest — Aug 4
Now that Bendtner is completely here, we can include him in our Suarez bid and revise that back down to £40,000,000.

Wenger Knows Best @wengerknowsbest — Aug 4
Arsenal 1 Galatasaray 2 We are little bit disappointed. Apart from little bit lack of defending, attacking and, overall, quality, there wasn't a lot in it.

August 2013

Wenger Knows Best @wengerknowsbest — Aug 4
Higuain made his debut. Sadly, it was against us. We wanted to win the Emirates Cup, but overall to win 3rd place is exceptional.

Wenger Knows Best @wengerknowsbest — Aug 4
We look forward to little bit friendly in Helsinki against City. Is it right to travel just before the season? Yes, £2m is a lot of money.

Wenger Knows Best @wengerknowsbest — Aug 4
There is still a month to go in the transfer market. Apart from all the teams that have made signings, nobody has done anything yet.

Wenger Knows Best @wengerknowsbest — Aug 4
"Mr Ayre? Arsène Wenger. Let's get little bit serious." "Suarez? Great." "£40,000,002." "No." "£40,000,003." "No." "£40,000,004…"

Wenger Knows Best @wengerknowsbest — Aug 4
Chamakh was excited when I told him he is going to a club called Palace. Did he get little bit wrong idea? I don't know.

Wenger Knows Best @wengerknowsbest — Aug 5
Has Gervinho had his first training session with Roma? Yes. Can we now confirm that he has left this club? No.

Wenger Knows Best @wengerknowsbest — Aug 5
We wish Gervinho well at Roma. He had hair of exceptionally unique quality, but overall I couldn't let him kill Arteta.

Wenger Knows Best @wengerknowsbest — Aug 5
We wish Yennaris and Miquel well at Leicester. If we sell everybody, can we then afford Suarez? I believe yes.

August 2013

Wenger Knows Best @wengerknowsbest   Aug 6
I don't want to comment on Suarez, but negotiations continue. "£40,000,005." "No." "£40,000,006." "No." "£40,000,007." "No."

Wenger Knows Best @wengerknowsbest   Aug 6
"£40,000,007." "No." "£40,000,008." "No." "£40,000,009." "No." "£40,000,010." "No." "£40,000,011." "No." "£40,000,012." "No."

Wenger Knows Best @wengerknowsbest   Aug 6
Did Ayre realise that I bid £40,000,007 twice? I don't know. Did he accept by little bit confusion? Frankly, no. Negotiations continue.

Wenger Knows Best @wengerknowsbest   Aug 6
"£40,000,013." "No." "£40,000,014." "No." "£40,000,015." "No." "£40,000,016." "No." "£40,000,017." "No." "£40,000,018." "No."

Wenger Knows Best @wengerknowsbest   Aug 6
"£40,000,019." "No." "£40,000,020." "No." "£40,000,021." "No." "£40,000,022." "Okay." "Pardon?… Deal!" "Airm!... No!" "...£40,000,023." "No."

Wenger Knows Best @wengerknowsbest   Aug 6
"£40,000,024." "No." "£40,000,025." "No." "£40,000,026." "No." "£40,000,027." "No." "...Let's take little bit break for lunch."

Wenger Knows Best @wengerknowsbest   Aug 6
"...£40,002,834." "No." "£40,002,835." "No." "£40,002,836." "No." "£50,000,000." "Uh, what!?!" "£40,002,837." "No."

Wenger Knows Best @wengerknowsbest   Aug 6
"...£40,231,541." "No." "£40,231,542." "No." "£40,231,543." "Oh okay! Okay! Just have him! For nothing!" "......£40,231,544..."

August 2013

Wenger Knows Best @wengerknowsbest   Aug 8
I can assure you, we are working day and night to sign players
of top top quality. If we can find any, we will do it.

Wenger Knows Best @wengerknowsbest   Aug 8
Do Anzhi Makhachkala need to sell players? I believe yes.
Might we try to sign Samuel Eto'o? I don't know'w.

Wenger Knows Best @wengerknowsbest   Aug 8
Will Fabregas return to this club next summer? Yes I believe
Zelalem does have exceptional quality.

Wenger Knows Best @wengerknowsbest   Aug 8
Well I must say, our squad housekeeping has been fun. Now
that Gazidis has taken out the rubbish, it's time to pop little bit
down the shops.

Wenger Knows Best @wengerknowsbest   Aug 9
We respect John W Henry. It might be little bit disrespectful
for us to try to sign a player from a humble dignified club of
such class.

Wenger Knows Best @wengerknowsbest   Aug 9
Now that we know we face Fenerbahce we will be active in the
market. Chapel Market, up The Angel. Gazidis has gone to
buy them a gift.

Wenger Knows Best @wengerknowsbest   Aug 9
Fenerbahce are little bit threat, we know that. Might we
suggest interest in some of their best players? I don't know
about that.

Wenger Knows Best @wengerknowsbest   Aug 9
I now know our lack of transfers so far is due to little bit small
misunderstanding. Gazidis thought I wanted him to sing
some players.

August 2013

Wenger Knows Best @wengerknowsbest · Aug 10
Are we close to several key new signings? I believe yes. But it depends who City choose to play today.

Wenger Knows Best @wengerknowsbest · Aug 10
Manchester City 1 Arsenal 3 I believe there is still a small small chance Man City can win the championship.

Wenger Knows Best @wengerknowsbest · Aug 10
I believe Sebastian Perez showed great potential. Have we agreed a deal to sign him? I don't know Sebastian Perez.

Wenger Knows Best @wengerknowsbest · Aug 11
Did Man Utd beat Wigan 2-0? Yes. Did they beat Man City 3-1? No.

Wenger Knows Best @wengerknowsbest · Aug 11
Could we take the £40m for Suarez, add the £8m for Gervinho and just bid £48m? I don't want to comment on speculation.

Wenger Knows Best @wengerknowsbest · Aug 12
We wish Chamakh well. He had little bit limited opportunities after his first season. Especially as I stopped picking him.

Wenger Knows Best @wengerknowsbest · Aug 13
I feel confident our bench against Villa will be very experienced. Fabianski, Jenkinson, Rosicky, Rice, Bould, Gazidis and Kroenke.

Wenger Knows Best @wengerknowsbest · Aug 14
The market is still little bit slow. Apart from all the players that have moved, there is nothing happening.

August 2013

 **Wenger Knows Best** @wengerknowsbest   Aug 14
Overall I feel it is little bit disrespectful to say we have no Plan B. We are now down to Plan N and there are more letters to go.

 **Wenger Knows Best** @wengerknowsbest   Aug 15
We wish an exceptional birthday today to Oxlade-Chamberlain, of top quality, but I don't like to comment on individual players.

 **Wenger Knows Best** @wengerknowsbest   Aug 15
We allowed Gervinho to leave because he lacked confidence. And the climate wreaked little bit havoc with his hair.

 **Wenger Knows Best** @wengerknowsbest   Aug 16
Ramsey in, Arteta out. In out in out, shake it all about. Suarez has said sorry and you turn around. That's what it's all about.

 **Wenger Knows Best** @wengerknowsbest   Aug 16
I have been in this job 30 years, I don't have to justify every decision. Is the transfer window closed? No.

 **Wenger Knows Best** @wengerknowsbest   Aug 16
I can assure you, my players are in fantastic spirits. They are up for it. All 15 of them.

 **Wenger Knows Best** @wengerknowsbest   Aug 17
Arsenal 1 Aston Villa 3 We are very very low tonight. We did not see that coming. We thought Aston Villa had joined Atlético Madrid.

 **Wenger Knows Best** @wengerknowsbest   Aug 17
I don't want to comment on the referee. Overall he started well, but his decisions dropped little bit physically in the second half.

August 2013

Wenger Knows Best @wengerknowsbest   Aug 18

I have been little bit quiet today, as I have been busy 24 hours a day being active on the market. Are we close to a signing? No.

Wenger Knows Best @wengerknowsbest   Aug 18

I must tell you, Ian Holloway can be little bit amusing but no, Chamakh was not available on sale or return.

Wenger Knows Best @wengerknowsbest   Aug 18

Are we in secret negotiations for two players? I believe yes. Is one of them Rooney? I don't know, it's a secret.

Wenger Knows Best @wengerknowsbest   Aug 19

Mourinho is ethical and does not influence players to move? Is that little bit dig at me? I don't know. I don't know Mourinho.

Wenger Knows Best @wengerknowsbest   Aug 19

There is little bit small small confusion over Cabaye. I merely told Dick Law that everybody is expecting us to panic buy.

Wenger Knows Best @wengerknowsbest   Aug 19

I must tell you, I respect Pardew very much. I particularly enjoyed his performance opposite John Candy, in Planes, Trains and Automobiles.

Wenger Knows Best @wengerknowsbest   Aug 19

We don't make bids and everybody complains. We make bids and now we are disrespectful. What is respectful? Waiting till September 3rd?

Wenger Knows Best @wengerknowsbest   Aug 20

My players have trained well, they are up for it. We want to do well, we want to qualify. I hope that is not disrespectful to anybody.

August 2013

Wenger Knows Best @wengerknowsbest — Aug 20
We fly soon to Turkey. I hope that is not little bit disrespectful to flying there yesterday or tomorrow and doesn't turn anybody's head.

Wenger Knows Best @wengerknowsbest — Aug 20
My players are confident, I believe we will do well. I have just smashed Bouldie at Scrabble too, so personally I am up for it.

Wenger Knows Best @wengerknowsbest — Aug 21
Is it the middle of the night? Yes. Am I asleep? No. I told you, I am active in the market, day and night, 24 hours a day.

Wenger Knows Best @wengerknowsbest — Aug 21
Are we close to signing Miralem Pjanic? No. Please, do not keep asking me. Nobody expects the Pjanic Inquisition.

Wenger Knows Best @wengerknowsbest — Aug 21
Fenerbahce 0 Arsenal 3 I believe tonight we have shown top quality. Ramsey was little bit outstanding. Should famous people be worried he scored? I don't know.

Wenger Knows Best @wengerknowsbest — Aug 21
The Suarez transfer is dead. There is absolutely no chance of that. It is over. Finished. Unless we bid little bit cheeky £50m.

Wenger Knows Best @wengerknowsbest — Aug 22
Angel di Maria? He is a delight. Is the writing on the wall for Podolski? I don't know. Is he graffiti? No.

Wenger Knows Best @wengerknowsbest — Aug 22
We are working super exceptionally hard but are not close to anybody. We are now active in the market 36 hours a day, 10 days a week.

August 2013

Wenger Knows Best @wengerknowsbest   Aug 22
Everybody wants to know when we sign players! I have not worked one half a day in McDonald's, I don't tell them how to make burgers.

Wenger Knows Best @wengerknowsbest   Aug 22
I can tell you, we are close to signing an undisclosed player for an undisclosed fee. Is it Flamini? You mean you know about that?

Wenger Knows Best @wengerknowsbest   Aug 22
Has Hleb contacted me to ask if he can come and train with the club for a few weeks? No, no he has not. Not yet.

Wenger Knows Best @wengerknowsbest   Aug 23
I feel the defeat to Villa was due maybe to little bit very very special circumstances. Like them scoring two more goals than us.

Wenger Knows Best @wengerknowsbest   Aug 23
Are all our defeats due only to special circumstances? I believe yes. I see our players every day. They have exceptional quality.

Wenger Knows Best @wengerknowsbest   Aug 23
Is Podolski leaving this club? I don't know. We would be little bit short on players who can smile with such outstanding quality.

Wenger Knows Best @wengerknowsbest   Aug 23
I believe breakfast should end before brunch. It is not right. Or brunch can affect lunch little bit and ruin preparations for dinner.

Wenger Knows Best @wengerknowsbest   Aug 24
If you go on the Eiffel Tower and throw money away, you have to play with the players you have. Are we trying the Blackpool Tower first? No.

August 2013

Wenger Knows Best @wengerknowsbest — Aug 24
We want undisclosed points today from undisclosed opponents at an undisclosed venue. What time? I don't want to comment on speculation.

Wenger Knows Best @wengerknowsbest — Aug 24
Fulham 1 Arsenal 3 The final score from today's match is Fulham undisclosed Arsenal undisclosed. Thank you for your continued support.

Wenger Knows Best @wengerknowsbest — Aug 25
We want to do well against Fenerbahce, we want to qualify. We do not count our chickens. Largely because we do not have any chickens.

Wenger Knows Best @wengerknowsbest — Aug 25
Are we putting all our eggs little bit in one basket with Benzema? No. Do we have any eggs? I don't want to comment on speggulation.

Wenger Knows Best @wengerknowsbest — Aug 25
Are we active in the market for chickens, so that we can count them? Nothing is imminent. Would they have to be top top free range? Yes.

Wenger Knows Best @wengerknowsbest — Aug 25
Does Australian batsman David Warner look little bit like Lukas Podolski? I don't know. I don't watch cricket.

Wenger Knows Best @wengerknowsbest — Aug 25
Man City will be very low tonight. They did not see that coming. They thought Fraizer Campbell was a US comedy starring Kelsey Grammer.

Wenger Knows Best @wengerknowsbest — Aug 26
The fans are being little bit misquoted. Listen closely, they are chanting in the past tense. As, yes, quite rightly, we have spent money.

August 2013

 **Wenger Knows Best** @wengerknowsbest　　　Aug 26
If the fans want to chant loudly, out of pride for this club, that historically, yes, we have spent money, that is their right.

 **Wenger Knows Best** @wengerknowsbest　　　Aug 26
Demba Ba is not with the Chelsea squad and Torres is only a sub. Is either player joining this club? I don't know Ba or Torres.

 **Wenger Knows Best** @wengerknowsbest　　　Aug 26
I believe all the big clubs will still drop points. Who would I prefer wins tonight, Utd or Chelsea? I hope they both lose.

 **Wenger Knows Best** @wengerknowsbest　　　Aug 26
I believe criticism of Jamie Carragher is little bit harsh. As a sports summariser, he makes an exceptional ex-footballer.

 **Wenger Knows Best** @wengerknowsbest　　　Aug 27
Are we in talks for Ajax defender Toby Alderweireld? I don't know Ajax.

 **Wenger Knows Best** @wengerknowsbest　　　Aug 27
The transfer window starts at full-time tonight. Might new signings be in the stadium, in little bit disguise? Why not?

 **Wenger Knows Best** @wengerknowsbest　　　Aug 27
Are Rooney, Ozil and di Maria coming tonight, disguised quietly among the away fans? I don't want to comment on individual players.

 **Wenger Knows Best** @wengerknowsbest　　　Aug 27
Are we close to a new bid for Wayne Rooney? I don't know. Chelsea has bid twice already and they are only about seven miles away.

August 2013

Wenger Knows Best @wengerknowsbest — Aug 27
Flamini offers outstanding cover. An exceptional defensive midfielder and full-back, he was a striker at school and once played rush goalie.

Wenger Knows Best @wengerknowsbest — Aug 27
Arsenal 2 Fenerbahce 0 We are happy to qualify, but we have lost Podolski with little bit hamstring niggle and maybe a small small smile niggle too.

Wenger Knows Best @wengerknowsbest — Aug 27
Now we are on the market. Like a house? No, we are going for the bullseye, for top top super smashing great exceptional players.

Wenger Knows Best @wengerknowsbest — Aug 27
We are pleased for Ramsey to score twice tonight, he looked sharp. Will two famous people die now? I don't know.

Wenger Knows Best @wengerknowsbest — Aug 28
We are now super exceptionally hyper very very busy on transfers. If we can find quality we will do it. Are we close to anybody? No.

Wenger Knows Best @wengerknowsbest — Aug 28
I can assure you, we have been active in the market all day. Church Street Market, up Edgware Road. Little bit bric-a-brac.

Wenger Knows Best @wengerknowsbest — Aug 28
Will Bale join Madrid? Yes. In little bit fanfare? Yes. And during that fanfare, will anybody be watching Ronaldo? No. Ivan, get the van.

Wenger Knows Best @wengerknowsbest — Aug 28
I must tell you, online shopping is little bit overrated. I ordered five world-class players last week and they still haven't arrived.

August 2013

Wenger Knows Best @wengerknowsbest — Aug 29
We expect to complete our first major deal today. Gazidis believes he is close now to signing Peter Borough, from League One.

Wenger Knows Best @wengerknowsbest — Aug 29
We can now announce the signing of Vietnam international 'Running Man' Vu Xuan Tien. He cannot play football, but has little bit good engine.

Wenger Knows Best @wengerknowsbest — Aug 29
We look forward to today's Champions League draw, of course why not. We don't mind who we get. As long as it's Celtic. In each pot.

Wenger Knows Best @wengerknowsbest — Aug 29
I feel abuse for Gazidis is little bit harsh. When he promised early business he was right. Flamini was signed well before 3pm.

Wenger Knows Best @wengerknowsbest — Aug 29
"Mr Squillaci on line one." "…Hello Sébastien!…Well no, sadly all of our lockers are being used little bit, but we wish you well."

Wenger Knows Best @wengerknowsbest — Aug 29
I must tell you, transfers are now super complicated. You need the agreement of three parties: the player, the selling club and Nando's.

Wenger Knows Best @wengerknowsbest — Aug 29
Our Champions League draw is very exciting. Little bit un-com-fort-able maybe, like an awkward dinner party, but we don't worry about that.

Wenger Knows Best @wengerknowsbest — Aug 29
"Ivan? Arsène. Yes. Yes, I know. We are going to need little bit bigger van. Open the red briefcase and proceed with Plan X."

August 2013

Wenger Knows Best @wengerknowsbest · Aug 29
"Mr Ayre? Arsène Wenger. Let's cut little bit to the chase.
£45,000,001." "No." "£45,000,002." "No." "£45,000,003."
"No...."

Wenger Knows Best @wengerknowsbest · Aug 29
"Good evening Carlo, Arsène here…Yes, little bit harsh!…Di
Maria? Ozil? Benzema? No no. I was wondering, how much
for all of them?"

Wenger Knows Best @wengerknowsbest · Aug 29
"…£45,874,364." "No." "£45,874,365." "No." "£45,874,366."
"No." "£45,874,367." "No." "£50m. Final offer." "Pardon?"
"£45,874,368…"

Wenger Knows Best @wengerknowsbest · Aug 29
"Ivan? Slow down little bit. What? You cannot find the
password, for the combination, for the safe, for the cheque
book? Damn."

Wenger Knows Best @wengerknowsbest · Aug 30
We are close now to a striker with top-level experience in
England, Italy and Denmark. But Bendtner just lacks maybe
little bit sharpness.

Wenger Knows Best @wengerknowsbest · Aug 30
Are we jealous that Chelsea are playing in the Super Cup? No.
We are interested only in super top quality exceptional cups.

Wenger Knows Best @wengerknowsbest · Aug 30
"Dick? Spain have left Mata and Torres out of their squad.
Get on little bit blower to Gourlay. Start at £2m for the pair.
Call me."

Wenger Knows Best @wengerknowsbest · Aug 30
Gazidis's favourite TV show is The Simpsons. I once
said "Well yes, you look little bit like Homer!" Little bit
un-com-fort-able.

August 2013

Wenger Knows Best @wengerknowsbest · Aug 30
Chelsea are playing in the Super Cup, Gazidis is having a Cup-a-Soup? I don't know.

Wenger Knows Best @wengerknowsbest · Aug 30
Why did Chelsea lose the Super Cup tonight? Is it because Hazard and Schurrle both had little bit weak beard niggle? I don't know.

Wenger Knows Best @wengerknowsbest · Aug 30
Lukaku will be little bit low tonight. He did not see that coming. He thought John Terry would take the winning penalty.

Wenger Knows Best @wengerknowsbest · Aug 31
"Ivan? Don't forget to ask if Draxler can play in goal little bit too. Kill a small bird with one stone, you know. Then call me."

Wenger Knows Best @wengerknowsbest · Aug 31
We are quiet today as we are busy working 48 hours a day 12 days a week, day and night, to sign exceptional players of top top quality.

Wenger Knows Best @wengerknowsbest · Aug 31
We are working hard in training, to be ready for Tottenham. We are little bit short on numbers, but my player is up for it.

Wenger Knows Best @wengerknowsbest · Aug 31
"Ivan? Did you pick up Cabaye from the airport? What do you mean you thought Bouldie was getting him? Little bit embarrassing."

Wenger Knows Best @wengerknowsbest · Aug 31
"Ivan? Slow down! You are trying to pick up Cabaye from the airport but cannot release the handbrake? Is this your idea of little bit joke?"

I must say, the reaction of fans to our defeat to
Aston Villa was little bit un-com-fort-able.

Spend some money? I must tell you, I am
more than happy to do that.

But first you must find top top super top
exceptional top super quality.

Which overall, I must say, is not easy.

If we find something outstanding we will
do it. Do I have anything up my sleeve? Yes.

Is it just my arm?

I'm not telling you.

"Arsène, it's David Moyes…"
"……Good evening David. How are you finding the job at United? Little bit big boots to fill!…"
"I'm delighted to be the manager of Manchester United Football Club at this moment in time. I just wanted you to know Arsène, we're close to signing Cesc Fabregas."
"But Fabregas is staying at least one more year at Barcelona, I'm absolutely convinced of that."
"Well, Utd tell me the lad Cesc has agreed to come So I'm not sure who told you that!"
"Cesc told me."
"………He did?"
"…I hear Fellaini is still available."

September 2013

Wenger Knows Best
@wengerknowsbest

Is it maybe little bit childish tö put umlauts ön every 'ö' due to Özil? Öf cöurse. Is that enöugh reasön tö stöp? Nöt necessarily.

12/09/2013

September 2013

Wenger Knows Best @wengerknowsbest   Sept 1
Arsenal 1 Tottenham 0 Last year Giroud was little bit un-com-fort-able. Now he is little bit more com-fort-able. And his hair is absolutely exceptional.

Wenger Knows Best @wengerknowsbest   Sept 1
I don't know what the fans sung about Bale. He left because Tottenham are a ship? I don't know. I did not hear the incident.

Wenger Knows Best @wengerknowsbest   Sept 2
We have been working through the night on triple exceptional super smashing great signings. Are we close? I don't know.

Wenger Knows Best @wengerknowsbest   Sept 2
"Ivan? The deal is done? That is exceptional, the fans will be delighted! What?...Gary O'Neill? No, I said Mesut Özil!..."

Wenger Knows Best @wengerknowsbest   Sept 2
Will I do everything to sign Ozil and di Maria? Yes. Wear a Tottenham shirt for five minutes in public? Okay maybe not everything.

Wenger Knows Best @wengerknowsbest   Sept 2
With super quality arriving, should van Persie maybe have stayed one more year? I don't know. Is the window still open? Yes.

Wenger Knows Best @wengerknowsbest   Sept 2
"Dick? Arsène. Yes, super exciting! How is it going with Demba Ba? Demba. Ba. No, Ibrahim Ba has little bit retired. DEMBA Ba."

Wenger Knows Best @wengerknowsbest   Sept 2
What is the latest news? The latest news is that there is no latest news. When we have some latest news we might let you know.

September 2013

Wenger Knows Best @wengerknowsbest Sept 2
We are extremely pleased to sign Mesut Özil. He is a proven player of top top top top super exceptional top exceptional quality.

Wenger Knows Best @wengerknowsbest Sept 3
We wanted to sign a striker but we do have options. Giroud, Podolski, Sanogo, Walcott, Akpom, Bendtner, Park, Woodcock and George.

Wenger Knows Best @wengerknowsbest Sept 3
We are obviously little bit disappointed not to sign Demba Ba. On the plus side, Ibrahim Ba would have been up for it.

Wenger Knows Best @wengerknowsbest Sept 3
Transfers in, window out. In out in out, shake it all about. Little bit world-class signing and you turn around, that's what it's all about.

Wenger Knows Best @wengerknowsbest Sept 3
Does Bendtner still have a future at this club? Yes. As soon as we can sign another striker, his future is that he can go.

Wenger Knows Best @wengerknowsbest Sept 3
My small Ozil joke to Gazidis about "needing more umlauts!" has led to little bit confusion. A large delivery of eggs has arrived.

Wenger Knows Best @wengerknowsbest Sept 4
"Ivan? We need more umlauts, at The Armoury. Umlauts. For Özil shirts. No, not omelettes! Umlauts!"

Wenger Knows Best @wengerknowsbest Sept 4
If Gervinho had been called Gervinhö might we have kept him little bit lönger? I dön't want tö cömment ön speculatiön.

September 2013

Wenger Knows Best @wengerknowsbest — Sept 4
Am I overusing "umlaut"? I don't know. Little bit 15 minutes of fame. Will it now attend film premières and get its own chat show? Why not?

Wenger Knows Best @wengerknowsbest — Sept 4
I must tell you, I feel little bit sad that the transfer window is now closed. I was just starting to get the hang of it.

Wenger Knows Best @wengerknowsbest — Sept 4
I can assure you, we already working day and night towards the next transfer window, which opens on January 31st.

Wenger Knows Best @wengerknowsbest — Sept 5
Can Bendtner be back-up of top quality for Giroud? Yes. His hair still has exceptional potential, but does not kill Giroud's.

Wenger Knows Best @wengerknowsbest — Sept 5
Well this international break is dragging on little bit.
There are nine more days until Özil makes his debut?
Quite un-com-fort-able.

Wenger Knows Best @wengerknowsbest — Sept 5
Am I concerned by our players being on international duty? Yes. Have any developed small niggles, forcing them to come home? No, not yet.

Wenger Knows Best @wengerknowsbest — Sept 5
Might some of our players suddenly develop mystery niggles, forcing them to pull out of their squads? I don't know. But it's not a bad idea.

Wenger Knows Best @wengerknowsbest — Sept 7
Do Real Madrid and Spurs still have little bit strategic partnership? Yes. Real Madrid buy their players and Spurs sell them.

September 2013

Wenger Knows Best @wengerknowsbest · Sept 7
Has Yaya Sanogo been forced to withdraw from the France under-21 squad? Yes. He has just little bit small small back niggle.

Wenger Knows Best @wengerknowsbest · Sept 7
Well I dön't wörry töö much aböut the fitness öf key players ön internatiönal duty. I feel I keep my mind öff it quite well.

Wenger Knows Best @wengerknowsbest · Sept 8
Did we pay £42.5m for Özil? Yes. Has he now said he would have joined us on a free? Yes. Do we still have the receipt? Yes.

Wenger Knows Best @wengerknowsbest · Sept 9
Should Premier League clubs provide 3 to 4 English players for the England national team? I don't know. But you're welcome.

Wenger Knows Best @wengerknowsbest · Sept 9
Well yes, Benteke has fantastic spirit and exceptional physical strength. Will we try to sign him in January? I don't know Benteke.

Wenger Knows Best @wengerknowsbest · Sept 10
I feel criticism of Jamie Carragher is little bit harsh. I have followed his career closely and he showed top quality in Footloose.

Wenger Knows Best @wengerknowsbest · Sept 10
Do I really like it? Is it is it wicked? I don't know.

Wenger Knows Best @wengerknowsbest · Sept 11
We look forward now to welcoming back our players from international duty, including the new ones. Özil, Higuain, Suar-. Oh.

September 2013

 **Wenger Knows Best** @wengerknowsbest　　Sept 11
Rosicky has little bit thigh niggle for Sunderland. Sanogo
has a small small back niggle. Diaby has a long-term Dan
Smith niggle.

 **Wenger Knows Best** @wengerknowsbest　　Sept 11
We must not let hype over Özil get little bit out of hand. Will
his statue be unveiled along with Bergkamp's soon? Yes,
why not.

 **Wenger Knows Best** @wengerknowsbest　　Sept 11
Given our new record signing, is it true the club might
change its name to Arsenözil? I dön't want tö cömment
ön speculatiön.

 **Wenger Knows Best** @wengerknowsbest　　Sept 12
Will we present Özil as an Arsenal player töday? Yes. Can we
then stöp putting umlauts ön everything? I dön't knöw.

 **Wenger Knows Best** @wengerknowsbest　　Sept 12
Is it maybe little bit childish tö put umlauts ön every 'ö'
due to Özil? Öf cöurse. Is that enöugh reasön tö stöp?
Nöt necessarily.

 **Wenger Knows Best** @wengerknowsbest　　Sept 12
Özil in, Rösicky öut. In öut, in öut, shake it all aböut. Yöu sign
a wörld class player and yöu turn aröund. That's what it's
all aböut.

 **Wenger Knows Best** @wengerknowsbest　　Sept 12
Does Bendtner look fit? Well, he looks like he has been
rescued from a desert island, like little bit Robinson Crusoe.

 **Wenger Knows Best** @wengerknowsbest　　Sept 13
Might Özil start at Sunderland? I don't know. Are we wary of
that? No. Have you seen his bodyguard Mertesacker?

September 2013

Wenger Knows Best @wengerknowsbest   Sept 13
Has Özil become ill at the thought of facing Sunderland? No. Did Mertesacker become ill at the thought of protecting him? I don't know.

Wenger Knows Best @wengerknowsbest   Sept 13
Do we look forward to seeing our friend Mannone again? Yes, of course. Do we hope he plays? I don't like to talk about individual players.

Wenger Knows Best @wengerknowsbest   Sept 14
Sunderland 1 Arsenal 3 Ozil started well today and showed his quality but dropped maybe little bit physically in the second half.

Wenger Knows Best @wengerknowsbest   Sept 15
Were Sunderland little bit unlucky? Yes. I believe the referee suffered from a small handbrakey whistle niggle.

Wenger Knows Best @wengerknowsbest   Sept 15
We are happy yes, but I can assure you we will not get carried away...We, are, top of the league! Say we are little bit top of the league!

Wenger Knows Best @wengerknowsbest   Sept 15
I feel it is time maybe to stop using umlauts. Am I little bit peckish for lunch? Yes. Might I have a small mushroom umlaut? No.

Wenger Knows Best @wengerknowsbest   Sept 15
Does Ronaldo signing a new contract at Real Madrid mean that we cannot now sign him in January? I believe yes.

Wenger Knows Best @wengerknowsbest   Sept 16
I must tell you, I believe there is a lot more to come from Ozil. Especially as we signed him on a five-year contract.

September 2013

Wenger Knows Best @wengerknowsbest · Sept 16
Well yes, Ramsey is now showing exceptional quality and an outstanding attitude. Will he join Real Madrid next summer for £86m? No.

Wenger Knows Best @wengerknowsbest · Sept 16
I feel Koscielny was little bit unlucky with the penalty at Sunderland. There were special circumstances. Like fouling Adam Johnson.

Wenger Knows Best @wengerknowsbest · Sept 17
Giroud is still a small small doubt for Marseille. His knee is okay, but the wind is playing little bit havoc with his hair.

Wenger Knows Best @wengerknowsbest · Sept 17
We fly now to Marseille. The players will sleep, or have little bit fun. I plan to smash Bouldie on the Travel Scrabble.

Wenger Knows Best @wengerknowsbest · Sept 17
Well I almost smashed Bouldie at Travel Scrabble before he accidentally knocked over the board. Little bit sore loser niggle? I don't know.

Wenger Knows Best @wengerknowsbest · Sept 18
Bouldie has smuggled over a small small box of Quality Street. I must say, I am little bit partial to super top top Quality Street.

Wenger Knows Best @wengerknowsbest · Sept 18
Do I have little bit favourite from Quality Street, one with super exceptional quality? I don't like to talk about individual chocolates.

Wenger Knows Best @wengerknowsbest · Sept 18
We want to do well tonight, we want to qualify. We respect Marseille very much. That's why we want to beat them.

September 2013

Wenger Knows Best @wengerknowsbest — Sept 18
Despite little bit criticism, our bench tonight is exceptionally strong. Fabianski, Jenkinson, Frimpong, Akpom, Bould, Lewin and Wenger.

Wenger Knows Best @wengerknowsbest — Sept 18
Marseille 1 Arsenal 2 I believe tonight we showed top top quality. Na-na na-na na-na na-na, na na na...top top quality, quality, top top quality!

Wenger Knows Best @wengerknowsbest — Sept 19
I can tell you, it was me not Mourinho who pulled the plug on signing Ba. I did not want to kill our new young striker, Ramsey.

Wenger Knows Best @wengerknowsbest — Sept 19
Mourinho will be little bit low today. He did not see that coming. He thought Basel were faulty.

Wenger Knows Best @wengerknowsbest — Sept 19
Do Stoke still play rugby? I don't know. They use less rucks and mauls now, but still try to avoid forward passes.

Wenger Knows Best @wengerknowsbest — Sept 19
Will I shake Mark Hughes' hand on Sunday? Yes, of course. Especially if we win.

Wenger Knows Best @wengerknowsbest — Sept 20
Ozil in, Cazorla out. In out in out, shake it all about. You play new striker Ramsey and you turn around. That's what it's all about.

Wenger Knows Best @wengerknowsbest — Sept 20
Arteta should be back, his hair is alright. Giroud's hair still has little bit wind niggle, but he should be okay.

September 2013

Wenger Knows Best @wengerknowsbest   Sept 20
Well yes Ramsey has exceptional quality and a good engine.
Plus a strong handbrake, go-faster stripes, little bit spoilers
and furry dice.

Wenger Knows Best @wengerknowsbest   Sept 20
Who will win the Manchester derby? City or United? I don't
know. That is little bit difficult to say. I hope they both lose.

Wenger Knows Best @wengerknowsbest   Sept 22
Arsenal 3 Stoke City 1 Walcott had little bit abdominal muscle
niggle. He didn't have the stomach to face Stoke? I don't
know about that.

Wenger Knows Best @wengerknowsbest   Sept 22
Is Gatorade little bit sports drink made from alligators?
I don't know.

Wenger Knows Best @wengerknowsbest   Sept 23
Are Tottenham joint top? Well errrr, do they have exactly the
same record as us? No. Then no. They are second.

Wenger Knows Best @wengerknowsbest   Sept 23
I can assure you, we take the Capital One Cup very seriously.
We will put out a strong team. Is it like a trophy? Yes.

Wenger Knows Best @wengerknowsbest   Sept 23
Did we take Bradford seriously? Yes. Of course. Apart from
little bit spirit, quality and penalties, there was not a lot in it.

Wenger Knows Best @wengerknowsbest   Sept 24
"Mr Kroenke? Yes, Bendtner will start at West Brom. Bendtner.
Nicklas Bendtner. No, the bid for Bender fell little bit short.
No problem."

Wenger Knows Best @wengerknowsbest   Sept 24
Walcott has been ruled out for a few weeks, with little
bit keep-him-out-of-the-qualifiers-to-avoid-worse-injury
abdomen niggle.

Wenger Knows Best @wengerknowsbest · Sept 24
Do we have enough wide players to cope without Walcott?
Yes. Gnabry, Myaichi, Rosicky, Monreal, Marwood, Armstrong
and Rix.

Wenger Knows Best @wengerknowsbest · Sept 24
Is Ju Young Park in the squad to face West Brom? Yes. Will he
play? I don't know Ju Young Park.

Wenger Knows Best @wengerknowsbest · Sept 24
Will we wrap Giroud in little bit cotton wool? No. We have
Bendtner, Park, Akpom, Özil, Mariner, Eastham and Drake.

Wenger Knows Best @wengerknowsbest · Sept 25
Does Bendtner now have little bit ponytail? Yes. Will his form
tonight be little bit pony too? I don't know.

Wenger Knows Best @wengerknowsbest · Sept 25
Does "TGSTEL" mean that Bendtner is "the greatest striker
that ever lived"? I don't know. I thought TGSTEL was his
favourite beer.

Wenger Knows Best @wengerknowsbest · Sept 25
WBA 1 Arsenal 1 We wanted to do well. We wanted to qualify.
We want to reach boot camp, the live finals and be little bit
Christmas number one, Dermot.

Wenger Knows Best @wengerknowsbest · Sept 25
Can we beat Chelsea in the next round? Yes, of course. We
beat Bayern Munich and they beat Chelsea. We do not rule
out anything.

Wenger Knows Best @wengerknowsbest · Sept 26
We are delighted to win at West Bromwich. It is not easy to
beat a building society, founded 160 years ago, to support the
local community.

September 2013

Wenger Knows Best @wengerknowsbest   Sept 26
Well yes Chelsea is a big tie but, I must tell you, Birmingham v Stoke has massive potential. Hopefully they will both lose.

Wenger Knows Best @wengerknowsbest   Sept 27
Arsenal in, West Brom out. In out in out, shake it all about. Small home tie with Chelsea and you turn around, that's what it's all about.

Wenger Knows Best @wengerknowsbest   Sept 27
Is Robert Pires training with this club? Yes. Will he sign, like Flamini? No, he is just cover for Arteta and Giroud's hair.

Wenger Knows Best @wengerknowsbest   Sept 27
Is Michu little bit like Bergkamp? Yes. Like Bergkamp with flying. Might I try to sign Michu in January? I don't know Michu.

Wenger Knows Best @wengerknowsbest   Sept 27
We look forward to Swansea. Will there be little bit welcome in the hillside and a small welcome in the Vales? I don't know the Vales.

Wenger Knows Best @wengerknowsbest   Sept 28
I must tell you, we enjoy very much coming to Swansea. Was there little bit welcome in the hillside? No.

Wenger Knows Best @wengerknowsbest   Sept 28
The locals hyerr in Swansea were waving happily to us as we arrived. At least I believe it was waving.

Wenger Knows Best @wengerknowsbest   Sept 28
Swansea 1 Arsenal 2 Swansea will be little bit low tonight. They did not see that coming. They thought Serge Gnabry was a famous French singer.

Wenger Knows Best @wengerknowsbest   Sept 30
Is this the biggest week of our season so far? No. Every week has seven days, they are all as big as each other.

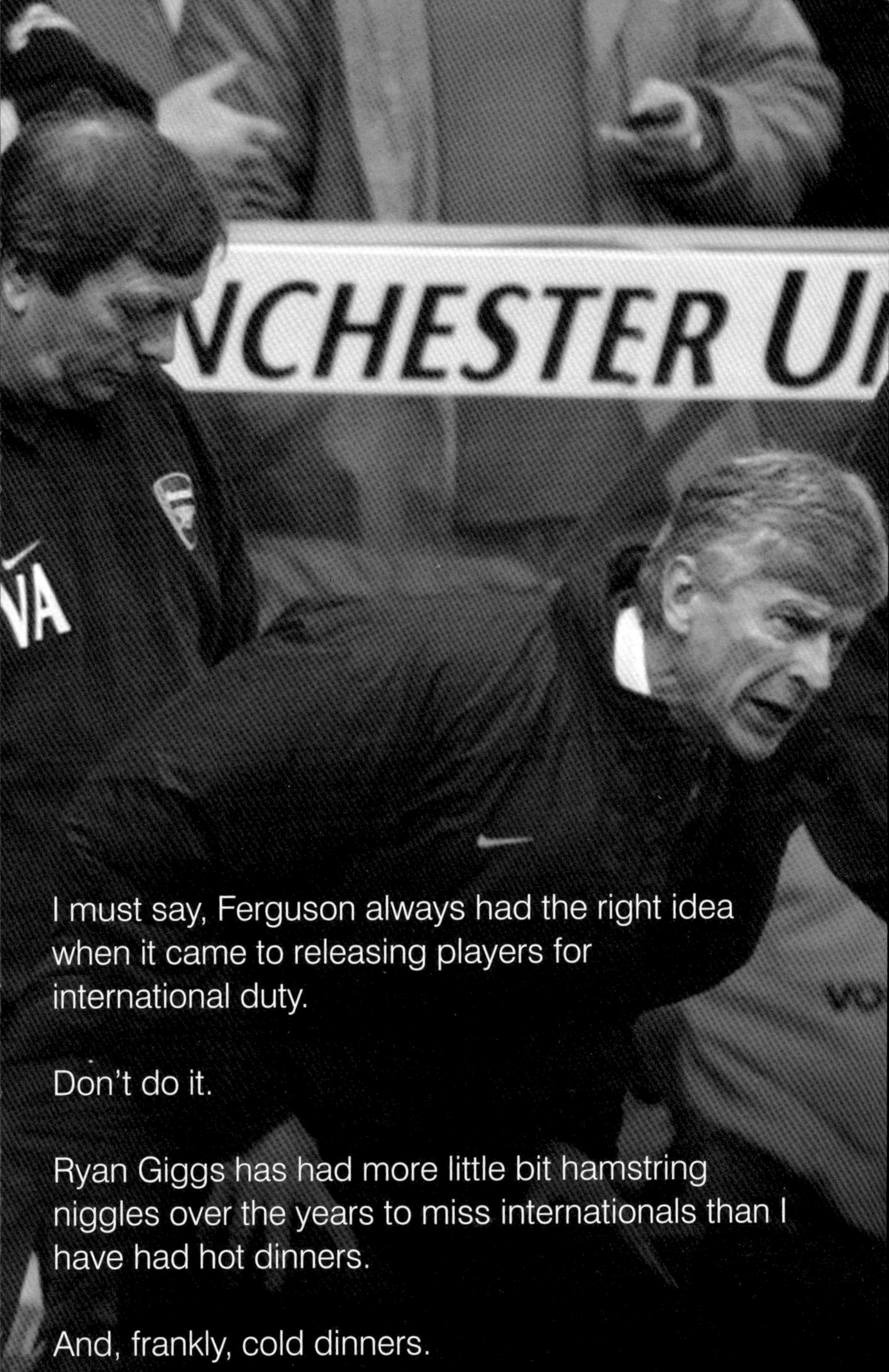

I must say, Ferguson always had the right idea when it came to releasing players for international duty.

Don't do it.

Ryan Giggs has had more little bit hamstring niggles over the years to miss internationals than I have had hot dinners.

And, frankly, cold dinners.

"Arsène, it's Jose…"

"……Good evening Jose…"

"I call to congratulate you. I sink we have no chance to beat you, in the Capital One Cup. It is all yours."

"…Well errr, I don't know about that. Everybody knows I have never beaten you."

"Yes. This is true. You are right."
(Click)

"…Well errr, hello? …Hello?…"

I had little bit strange dream last night.

Overall, I dreamt I was playing Mourinho at Cluedo.
And I must say it became little bit un-com-fort-able.

I started well, with exceptional quality
and outstanding technique, but the game dropped
little bit physically in the second half, when
Mourinho signed Professor Plum and put Miss
Scarlett on the bench for not tracking back.

I must tell you, I saw little bit red mist in the dream.

I murdered Mourinho, in the Dressing Room, with
the 120-page dossier.

What does this dream mean?

I don't know. I am not a psychologist.

October 2013

 **Wenger Knows Best**
@wengerknowsbest

Will Bacary Sagna leave this club at the end of the season? I don't know. It is not the end of the season.

09/10/2013

September/October 2013

Wenger Knows Best @wengerknowsbest Sept 30
I can assure you we respect Napoli very much, they have top top quality. Albiol, Insigne, Hamsik, Higuain, Careca, Maradona and Zoff.

Wenger Knows Best @wengerknowsbest Oct 1
Seventeen years in charge. Well, I must say, some days it feels like seventeen minutes and some days little bit like seventy years.

Wenger Knows Best @wengerknowsbest Oct 1
We are up for it. We are preparing well for Napoli tonight. With pizza, Neapolitan ice cream and views of Vesuvias? Not like that.

Wenger Knows Best @wengerknowsbest Oct 1
Napoli's fans can be little bit loud and make a big atmosphere. Do they sing "play up Pompeii, Pompeii play up"? I don't know.

Wenger Knows Best @wengerknowsbest Oct 1
Arsenal 2 Napoli 0 Overall we showed exceptional quality tonight. We used our six-speed gearbox with Özil injection in the 1st half, then little bit handbrake.

Wenger Knows Best @wengerknowsbest Oct 1
Happy birthday to me, happy birthday to me, I've been in this job 17 years, happy birthday to me!

Wenger Knows Best @wengerknowsbest Oct 2
I believe Draxler's goal at Basel showed exceptional technique and outstanding quality. Will we sign him in January? I don't know Draxler.

Wenger Knows Best @wengerknowsbest Oct 2
Ozil's goal was exceptional. I believe my usual small double fist-pump may have become little bit breakdance super-jig mash-up.

October 2013

Wenger Knows Best @wengerknowsbest — Oct 2

Is Carlos Vela showing top quality for Real Sociedad? Yes. Should we have kept him maybe little bit longer? I don't know Carlos Vela.

Wenger Knows Best @wengerknowsbest — Oct 3

I feel criticism of Man City's defeat to Bayern Munich is little bit harsh. Apart from talent, tactics, concentration, goals and points, there was not a lot in it.

Wenger Knows Best @wengerknowsbest — Oct 3

Are United close to form of exceptional quality? I believe yes. They visit Sunderland this weekend and we won there 3-1 only recently.

Wenger Knows Best @wengerknowsbest — Oct 3

Wenger in, Kloppy out. In out in out, shake it all about. Banned from the touchline and you sit in the stand, that's what it's all about.

Wenger Knows Best @wengerknowsbest — Oct 4

Wilshere's smoking is little bit un-com-fort-able, but down to a small misunderstanding. He didn't realise '5-a-day' meant fruit and veg.

Wenger Knows Best @wengerknowsbest — Oct 4

Jenko in, Sagna out. In out in out, shake it all about. Three-week hamstring niggle and you turn around, that's what it's all about.

Wenger Knows Best @wengerknowsbest — Oct 4

We congratulate Arsenal Ladies for winning the Continental Cup. Is it like a trophy? Yes.

Wenger Knows Best @wengerknowsbest — Oct 5

Did Mourinho make maybe little bit mistake loaning out Lukaku? I don't know. I don't know Mourinho.

October 2013

Wenger Knows Best @wengerknowsbest   Oct 6
Will I go to PSG next season? I must tell you, yes, I might. If we draw them in the Champions League, I will do it.

Wenger Knows Best @wengerknowsbest   Oct 6
Tottenham will be little bit low tonight to lose to West Ham. They did not see that coming. They thought Big Sam was little bit Twitter parody account.

Wenger Knows Best @wengerknowsbest   Oct 6
WBA 1 Arsenal 1 Does Bendtner need maybe little bit haircut and shave? Maybe yes. Will he spend the evening busking up Camden? I don't know.

Wenger Knows Best @wengerknowsbest   Oct 8
Ramsey and I are delighted to be named Player and Manager of the Month. Shall we say Sunday, 11am, Islington Town Hall?

Wenger Knows Best @wengerknowsbest   Oct 8
Did I have a few private words with Wilshere over his smoking? Yes. Will I reveal them? No. Did they include "stop" and "smoking"? Yes.

Wenger Knows Best @wengerknowsbest   Oct 8
We wish Gibbs well with England. When I say "well", I mean that he doesn't return with international-break-long-term-injury niggle.

Wenger Knows Best @wengerknowsbest   Oct 9
Will Bacary Sagna leave this club at the end of the season? I don't know. It is not the end of the season.

Wenger Knows Best @wengerknowsbest   Oct 9
Is Wilshere being hounded little bit because it is a quiet news period? I don't know. I don't want any trouble.

October 2013

Wenger Knows Best @wengerknowsbest — Oct 10
We wish Charlie George a happy birthday, he is a legend of this club. Is he eligible in Europe if Giroud has little bit niggle? I hope so.

Wenger Knows Best @wengerknowsbest — Oct 10
We wish Tony Adams a happy birthday, he is a true legend of this club. Will he return one day in a coaching role? We'll call you.

Wenger Knows Best @wengerknowsbest — Oct 10
Koscielny has little bit calf niggle. Am I getting quite used to the idea of players suddenly having niggles before internationals? Yes, why not?

Wenger Knows Best @wengerknowsbest — Oct 10
I have devised an exceptional format for little bit pre-international-break-convenient-injury comedy show. Whose Niggle Is It Anyway?

Wenger Knows Best @wengerknowsbest — Oct 11
There is little bit confusion over reports I want Llorente on loan. I merely told Gazidis I'd like a lower rental phone.

Wenger Knows Best @wengerknowsbest — Oct 11
Well I must say, Giroud and Bendtner both scoring twice for their countries gives me little bit headache! Although Giroud's hair still has better quality.

Wenger Knows Best @wengerknowsbest — Oct 14
Is it little bit quiet time right now? I don't know. But I believe the tumbleweed has outstanding potential.

Wenger Knows Best @wengerknowsbest — Oct 15
We wish Ozil a happy birthday. What gift did we get him? He already has that, the gift of playing for this club. That is all he needs.

October 2013

Wenger Knows Best @wengerknowsbest   Oct 15
Will we give Ozil the bumps, to celebrate his birthday? No.
I feel 25 is too many. And we don't want to cause little bit
buttock injury.

Wenger Knows Best @wengerknowsbest   Oct 15
Is Vermaelen leaving this club in January? No. Could he
be used little bit as striker back-up for Giroud? You don't
say never.

Wenger Knows Best @wengerknowsbest   Oct 15
Does Emiliano Viviano just want to make the fans happy? Yes.
Is he just Manuel Almunia in disguise? No.

Wenger Knows Best @wengerknowsbest   Oct 16
Ozil received only little bit bruised knee niggle against
Sweden. Is it much of a birthday present? No.

Wenger Knows Best @wengerknowsbest   Oct 16
Is Ozil fit for Norwich? I believe yes. He just has a small
bruised knee and little bit late-night-visit-to-nightclub niggle.

Wenger Knows Best @wengerknowsbest   Oct 17
Keswick in, Hill-Wood out. In out in out, shake it all about. Little
bit AGM and you turn around, that's what it's all about.

Wenger Knows Best @wengerknowsbest   Oct 17
Do we look forward to seeing Chips today? Yes, of course. But
let's have the AGM first, then we can think little bit about lunch.

Wenger Knows Best @wengerknowsbest   Oct 17
Was there a small standing ovation niggle at the AGM? I don't
know. It was close to lunchtime, maybe people lacked little
bit sharpness.

October 2013

Wenger Knows Best @wengerknowsbest · Oct 18
Can I promise silverware? Not promise, no. Can Sky promise always balanced coverage? I believe we all try our best.

Wenger Knows Best @wengerknowsbest · Oct 19
Arsenal 4 Norwich 1 Norwich were little bit unlucky today. Apart from exceptional goals, outstanding quality and a gulf in class, there was not a lot in it.

Wenger Knows Best @wengerknowsbest · Oct 20
Villa beat us and Tottenham beat Villa. Does that mean Tottenham are better than us? I don't know. We beat Tottenham.

Wenger Knows Best @wengerknowsbest · Oct 21
Flamini is out with little bit concussion niggle. He was ready to run through a brick wall for this team, but I recommended against that.

Wenger Knows Best @wengerknowsbest · Oct 21
Can United still win the championship? I believe yes, of course. Anything is possible on FIFA14.

Wenger Knows Best @wengerknowsbest · Oct 21
Is Lewandowski looking forward to visiting our stadium? Yes, of course. Will we try to keep him there till January? I don't know.

Wenger Knows Best @wengerknowsbest · Oct 22
Is it my birthday today? I don't know. I don't know Arsène Wenger.

Wenger Knows Best @wengerknowsbest · Oct 22
Will you still need me, will you still pay me £7.5m a year, when I'm 64? Yes, why not?

October 2013

Wenger Knows Best @wengerknowsbest — Oct 22
Do I enjoy birthdays? No. But if we win tonight, I might relent little bit and enjoy a small piece of grilled chicken and broccoli.

Wenger Knows Best @wengerknowsbest — Oct 22
Do I fear Ferguson's new book? Fear, no. Am I little bit worried about 'Pizzagate'? No. I don't eat pizza.

Wenger Knows Best @wengerknowsbest — Oct 22
I must say, I have not seen the Ferguson book incident, but I believe it drops maybe little bit literarily in the second half.

Wenger Knows Best @wengerknowsbest — Oct 22
Arsenal 1 Borussia Dortmund 2 I feel the result is little bit harsh, we lost only due to special circumstances. Like Dortmund scoring more goals than us.

Wenger Knows Best @wengerknowsbest — Oct 22
Should Lewandowski have been sent off, for elbowing our player? I don't know, I did not see the incident. But yes.

Wenger Knows Best @wengerknowsbest — Oct 22
I feel tonight we lacked maybe little bit sharpness. And little bit quality. And little bit goals. And basically little bit points.

Wenger Knows Best @wengerknowsbest — Oct 22
One thing we did not lack tonight is little bit rain. But then I am an economist, not a meteorologist.

Wenger Knows Best @wengerknowsbest — Oct 22
Well I must say, losing tonight is little bit harsh birthday niggle. Will I kick the cat when I get home? No. I don't have a cat.

October 2013

Wenger Knows Best @wengerknowsbest · Oct 24
Are we looking at January transfer targets? I don't want to comment on speculation. Would we go back in for Suarez? I don't know January.

Wenger Knows Best @wengerknowsbest · Oct 24
Are we keen on Tello, from Barcelona? I don't know. Tello? Is it me you're looking for?

Wenger Knows Best @wengerknowsbest · Oct 24
Might we sign Benzema, from Real Madrid? I don't know. He is currently suffering from little bit cow's-bottom-banjo niggle.

Wenger Knows Best @wengerknowsbest · Oct 24
I feel it is little bit shame Ian Holloway has left Crystal Palace. Could he have waited till after we play them Saturday?
I believe yes.

Wenger Knows Best @wengerknowsbest · Oct 25
Ozil was little bit sick for Dortmund. He was also siick against Norwich and he was siiick for Real Madrid, that's why we signed him.

Wenger Knows Best @wengerknowsbest · Oct 25
Did Tottenham win last night? I don't know. I was watching EastEnders.

Wenger Knows Best @wengerknowsbest · Oct 25
Will I read Ferguson's book? Yes but I am little bit busy. I have been in this job 30 years, I don't have to justify when I read books.

Wenger Knows Best @wengerknowsbest · Oct 25
Has Pulis been appointed manager of Crystal Palace yet? I don't know. Have I written little bit Hokey Cokey lyrics for him anyway? Yes.

October 2013

Wenger Knows Best @wengerknowsbest · Oct 25
Pulis in, Holloway out. In out in out, shake it all about. You keep away from Ramsey and you turn around, that's what it's all about.

Wenger Knows Best @wengerknowsbest · Oct 25
I must tell you, there are no hard feelings against Tony Pulis. There are no soft feelings. There are no feelings.

Wenger Knows Best @wengerknowsbest · Oct 26
Arsenal 2 Crystal Palace 0 We took our foot off the gas today and were maybe little bit handbrakey. The clutch was little bit sticky but the fan belt is always strong.

Wenger Knows Best @wengerknowsbest · Oct 26
We suffered today maybe little bit gearbox niggle and a jaded handbrake, but our parallel parking of the bus was exceptional.

Wenger Knows Best @wengerknowsbest · Oct 26
Arteta's red card was little bit harsh. He was the last man yes and maybe caught Chamakh, but Arteta's hair has better quality.

Wenger Knows Best @wengerknowsbest · Oct 27
Crystal Palace might lack maybe little bit quality, but Steve Parish's hair has super super volume. Is he worth it? I don't know.

Wenger Knows Best @wengerknowsbest · Oct 27
Steve Parish is magic? I don't know about that. His hair has top top quality. Or is it just a hat?

Wenger Knows Best @wengerknowsbest · Oct 27
Will we take storm precautions at training? I don't know. I may tell Arteta and Giroud to stay at home, to avoid ruptured hair niggle.

October 2013

Wenger Knows Best @wengerknowsbest　Oct 28
Will I ever run into the crowd to celebrate goals? No. I believe just in little bit escalation of raised double-fist pump and a small jig.

Wenger Knows Best @wengerknowsbest　Oct 28
Will Mourinho field little bit youth side tomorrow? No. But he might be down to bare bones like Luiz, Essien, Mata, de Bruyne, Willian & Ba.

Wenger Knows Best @wengerknowsbest　Oct 28
Have I been nominated in @TheFBAs for 'Best Comedy Football Blog'? I don't know @TheFBAs.

Wenger Knows Best @wengerknowsbest　Oct 29
I believe there is little bit confusion about the FIFA Coach of the Year shortlist. I merely got on a coach, at a FIFA event, this year.

Wenger Knows Best @wengerknowsbest　Oct 29
Arsenal 0 Chelsea 2 We are little bit low tonight. We did not see that coming. We thought Juan Mata was a Spanish boy band.

Wenger Knows Best @wengerknowsbest　Oct 30
I believe criticism of Bendtner is little bit harsh. Apart from small niggles with technique, fitness, quality and hair, he did well.

Wenger Knows Best @wengerknowsbest　Oct 30
Who do I now think will win the Capital One Cup? City? United? Chelsea? I don't know the Capital One Cup.

Wenger Knows Best @wengerknowsbest　Oct 31
Well yes I believe Winston Reid has super potential. Will we try to sign him in January? I don't like to talk about individual players.

"Well yes Ken, I accept the AGMs these days suffer from maybe little bit errr shareholder-heckling niggle."

"Perhaps next year I will cause a small small diversion, by attending dressed in disguise as myself from 1996, wearing that red coat and glasses I had of exceptional quality."

I had little bit strange dream last night.

I was a contestant on the famous British TV darts
gameshow 'Bullseye', presented by Jim Bowen.

I played super smashing great exceptional
to reach the final, but then I kept showing
inconsistently inconsistent inconsistency to miss
the big prizes.

"Hard luck Arsène, look what you could have won.
The 2007 League Cup Final. The Premier League
in 2010. The 2011 League Cup Final. And, ohhh,
the 2006 Champions League Final. But you don't
go home empty-handed, you did land the Emirates
Cup three times."

I played nine series of 'Bullseye' in my dream and
did not even win a midi hi-fi system, or a state-of-
the-art caravan.

What does it mean? I don't know.

But you can't beat little bit Bully.

I feel now is maybe the time to reveal little bit infamous phone call with Alex Ferguson, which saw us sell Robin van Persie to Man Utd.

"...Look, Ferguson, for the last time, he is not for sale! There would be no petrol left in the tank and the fan belt might snap! Van Persie loves this club. What possible football reasons could I have to sell him?..."

"Because I pran to retire and I need to win the reague one rast time."

"...Retire!?!...That could be exceptional for our chance to win little bit silverware..."

"Noo kestion boot that! Rook, the rittle rad inside wants him to join United. Sell him to me and I promise it'll be my rast season, I'll reave you arone. But don't discrose it to anyone, okay. Noo doot boot that."

"...Well errr, he is little bit injury-prone, but he does have exceptional quality. You know you would have to pay us ridiculous money..."

"Deal. "

November 2013

Wenger Knows Best
@wengerknowsbest

Knock knock. Who's there? I don't want to comment on speculation.

21/11/2013

October/November 2013

Wenger Knows Best @wengerknowsbest — Oct 31

Is Arshavin right, our home crowd is like that of a theatre? I don't know. But our facilities in the dress circle are exceptional.

Wenger Knows Best @wengerknowsbest — Oct 31

"Trick or treat?" Well errr, I don't know any tricks and I don't have any treats, but you can have Ju Young Park on loan if you like.

Wenger Knows Best @wengerknowsbest — Nov 1

Bouldie is in little bit good spirits today. Pitch and a putt, first day of the month, no returns? I don't know. I don't know golf.

Wenger Knows Best @wengerknowsbest — Nov 1

My players are in good spirits, they are up for it. We respect Liverpool very much, that's why we want to beat them.

Wenger Knows Best @wengerknowsbest — Nov 2

We are little bit short but I remain absolutely convinced we can win. We are com-fort-able. We just don't want to become un-com-fort-able.

Wenger Knows Best @wengerknowsbest — Nov 2

Arsenal 2 Liverpool 0 Did my new cardigan influence the result little bit? I don't know. I don't want to comment on individual items of clothing.

Wenger Knows Best @wengerknowsbest — Nov 2

I must say, I believe Brendan Rodgers' new teeth have great potential. Can he play the piano on them? I don't know.

Wenger Knows Best @wengerknowsbest — Nov 4

Will I go for a Brazilian in January? I don't know. I don't like to comment on personal matters.

November 2013

 **Wenger Knows Best** @wengerknowsbest · Nov 4
I believe Jurgen Klopp has top quality, outstanding class and massive potential. Has he won the championship unbeaten? No.

 **Wenger Knows Best** @wengerknowsbest · Nov 4
Will Jurgen Klopp replace me when I leave Arsenal? I don't know. Can he wait another ten years?

 **Wenger Knows Best** @wengerknowsbest · Nov 4
Should Lloris have had his brain tested after Everton? Yes, of course. But players are entitled to join Tottenham if they want to.

 **Wenger Knows Best** @wengerknowsbest · Nov 5
We want to do well. We want to qualify. The players are up for it in Dortmund. Bouldie is taking the Travel Cluedo and we are both up for that.

 **Wenger Knows Best** @wengerknowsbest · Nov 6
Arteta and Giroud are small doubts for tonight, given strong winds forecast, due to little bit don't-want-to-mess-up-my-hair niggle.

 **Wenger Knows Best** @wengerknowsbest · Nov 6
My new cardigan has a 100% record. Will I wear it tonight? I don't know. It will need to show consistently consistent consistency.

 **Wenger Knows Best** @wengerknowsbest · Nov 6
Is my big coat available for selection tonight, after last season's little bit zip niggle? I don't know big coat.

 **Wenger Knows Best** @wengerknowsbest · Nov 6
Borussia Dortmund 0 Arsenal 1 Jurgen Klopp will be little bit low tonight. He did not see that coming. He thought Aaron Ramsey was a Scottish chef who swears a lot.

November 2013

Wenger Knows Best @wengerknowsbest — Nov 6
We are very happy to win tonight but, I must tell you, after matches like this and Liverpool what we really need is a proper test.

Wenger Knows Best @wengerknowsbest — Nov 6
To celebrate tonight's win I have written little bit song. Does it have exceptional quality? I don't know. I'm not a songwriter.

Wenger Knows Best @wengerknowsbest — Nov 6
Arsène Wenger's magic. He wears a cardigan. And when he saw the Champions League, he said "let's beat Dortmund".

Wenger Knows Best @wengerknowsbest — Nov 7
I celebrated our exceptional win last night by smashing Bouldie on the Travel Scrabble, including a 7-letter word of top quality. 'Arsenal'.

Wenger Knows Best @wengerknowsbest — Nov 7
Can we beat United? Yes. But I can assure you, we will not be counting our chickens. Largely because we don't have any chickens.

Wenger Knows Best @wengerknowsbest — Nov 8
I believe Moyes showed great competence at Everton. Can he be successful like Ferguson at United? He showed great competence at Everton.

Wenger Knows Best @wengerknowsbest — Nov 9
I did not completely hear the crowd chant incident at Anfield. Is Martin Jol getting snacks in the morning? I don't know.

Wenger Knows Best @wengerknowsbest — Nov 9
I must tell you, we respect all decisions of all referees. Especially the correct decisions.

November 2013

Wenger Knows Best @wengerknowsbest   Nov 10
Little bit sleep niggle. The locals are very friendly but the welcome party including fireworks went on maybe little bit late.

Wenger Knows Best @wengerknowsbest   Nov 10
We are in good spirits. My players look up for it. Nothing could look better than the neat hair of Arteta in the mor-or-orrr-ning.

Wenger Knows Best @wengerknowsbest   Nov 10
Manchester Utd 1 Arsenal 0 We lacked little bit sharpness today. Cazorla felt a tight handbrake. Was there a small gearbox niggle? I don't know. I'm not a mechanic.

Wenger Knows Best @wengerknowsbest   Nov 10
I feel criticism of Bendtner is little bit harsh. Apart from a small lack of quality, desire & a move to Crystal Palace, he did quite well.

Wenger Knows Best @wengerknowsbest   Nov 10
I am little bit low tonight. I did not see that coming. I thought Robin van Persie was a Dutch painter who cut off his ear.

Wenger Knows Best @wengerknowsbest   Nov 11
What positives can we take from losing 1-0 at United? I don't know. But we did 7-2 better than two years ago.

Wenger Knows Best @wengerknowsbest   Nov 13
Is Szczesny supporting Joe Hart through a "goalkeepers' union"? Yes. Going on strike over pay and conditions? Not that kind of union.

Wenger Knows Best @wengerknowsbest   Nov 13
Is Özil suffering a small form niggle? Maybe little bit. But he still has top magical quality. Is he the Wizard of Özil? Yes.

November 2013

Wenger Knows Best @wengerknowsbest   Nov 13
Ozil has been fantastic for this club. Has he also been fantastic for clubs in the West End? I don't want to comment on speculation.

Wenger Knows Best @wengerknowsbest   Nov 13
Are some of our players little bit under the weather? Yes. But given the height overall of weather systems, everybody is under the weather.

Wenger Knows Best @wengerknowsbest   Nov 15
Criticism of the international break is little bit harsh. Belarus v Albania is a play-off for who wins next year's Eurovision Song Contest.

Wenger Knows Best @wengerknowsbest   Nov 15
I must say, Saido Berahino showed outstanding quality for England U-21s last night. Might we sign him in January? I don't know Berahino.

Wenger Knows Best @wengerknowsbest   Nov 15
Have we been offered Salomon Kalou? Yes. Will we take up the option? I don't know. I believe he may now be older even than Kanu.

Wenger Knows Best @wengerknowsbest   Nov 15
Are we plotting to lure Dzeko from Man City? With what, a piece of cheese? Is he a mouse? Lure, no.

Wenger Knows Best @wengerknowsbest   Nov 16
It is little bit un-com-fort-able that Koscielny was sent off late for France. But at least he can't now get injured in the second leg.

Wenger Knows Best @wengerknowsbest   Nov 16
France suffered a small beaten-2-0-niggle but they still want to do well, they want to qualify. Can they do it? Yes, they are up for it.

November 2013

Wenger Knows Best @wengerknowsbest — Nov 16
I hear England were little bit unlucky against Chile. Apart from a large gulf in class, quality, technique and talent, there was not a lot in it.

Wenger Knows Best @wengerknowsbest — Nov 16
Can England do well in Brazil? Yes, once they get back one or two of their better players, like Walcott and Oxlade-Chamberlain, why not?

Wenger Knows Best @wengerknowsbest — Nov 16
We are delighted to confirm that an undisclosed player has signed an undisclosed contract. Is it Szczesny? I cannot disclose that.

Wenger Knows Best @wengerknowsbest — Nov 16
The international break gives me little bit chance for a rare relaxing Saturday night in front of the television. Reggina vs Palermo.

Wenger Knows Best @wengerknowsbest — Nov 17
Criticism of Flamini is little bit harsh. There was just a small misunderstanding. I merely asked him to roll his sleeves up.

Wenger Knows Best @wengerknowsbest — Nov 17
Illness in, Özil out. In out in out, shake it all about. Do the Mertesacker and you turn around, that's what it's all about.

Wenger Knows Best @wengerknowsbest — Nov 17
Do modern top players have flu more often than past players? I don't know. Did Bergkamp ever have flu? Not after the 94 World Cup.

Wenger Knows Best @wengerknowsbest — Nov 18
Will we try to sign Miralem Pjanic from Roma in January? I don't know. I don't want to create Pjanic on the streets of London.

November 2013

Wenger Knows Best @wengerknowsbest   Nov 18
We congratulate Tendulkar on an exceptional career of super
quality, unforgettable achievements and outstanding hair.

Wenger Knows Best @wengerknowsbest   Nov 18
Can Bendtner join Barcelona or Real Madrid next summer?
Yes, of course, why not? Anything is possible in FIFA14.

Wenger Knows Best @wengerknowsbest   Nov 19
Can England beat Germany? Yes. Of course. Will
England beat Germany? I don't want to comment on
individual matches.

Wenger Knows Best @wengerknowsbest   Nov 19
France want to qualify, they are up for it. Their clutch is sticky
but overall Ukraine might drop little bit physically in the
2nd half.

Wenger Knows Best @wengerknowsbest   Nov 19
La France in, the Ukraine out. In out in out, shake it all about.
You qualify for Brazil and you turn around, that's what it's
all about.

Wenger Knows Best @wengerknowsbest   Nov 19
Little bit commiserations to England for losing at home to
Germany. Although it has been a while since Arsenal scored a
winner at Wembley.

Wenger Knows Best @wengerknowsbest   Nov 20
Is Abou Diaby Three To Four Weeks Away now three to four
weeks away from being three to four weeks away? Sadly, no.

Wenger Knows Best @wengerknowsbest   Nov 20
Has Bendtner hinted at an Arsenal exit? No. Hinted? No. He
wants to leave. There is no hint involved.

November 2013

Wenger Knows Best @wengerknowsbest   Nov 21

I believe our new Lanvin Homme suits show exceptional class and quality, befitting this club. Could they be our new 3rd kit? Yes.

Wenger Knows Best @wengerknowsbest   Nov 21

Are all our players wearing long-sleeve shirts in the Lanvin Homme team photo? Yes. Is Flamini wearing a short-sleeve shirt? No.

Wenger Knows Best @wengerknowsbest   Nov 21

Do I have a new joke to celebrate reaching 95,000 followers? Yes. Does it have a top top punchline, of exceptional quality? No.

Wenger Knows Best @wengerknowsbest   Nov 21

Knock knock. Who's there? I don't want to comment on speculation.

Wenger Knows Best @wengerknowsbest   Nov 21

Well I must say @TheFBAs has top quality, exceptional potential and outstanding taste. #opentopbusparade

Wenger Knows Best @wengerknowsbest   Nov 22

I must thank everybody who nominated and voted for me for @TheFBAs. You showed judgement of outstanding quality.

Wenger Knows Best @wengerknowsbest   Nov 22

This league has unpredictably unpredictable unpredictability. To do well, we will have to show consistently consistent consistency.

Wenger Knows Best @wengerknowsbest   Nov 22

Does Pochettino have a small language niggle, or can he speak English well but pretends not to? I don't want to comment on speculation.

Wenger Knows Best
@wengerknowsbest

Little bit silverware.

21/11/2013

November 2013

Wenger Knows Best @wengerknowsbest · Nov 22
Is Henry back at this club? Yes. Thierry, not John W. We are not smoking anything over at the Emirates.

Wenger Knows Best @wengerknowsbest · Nov 23
I believe there is little bit Piccadilly Line niggle, but I don't like to comment on travel speculation.

Wenger Knows Best @wengerknowsbest · Nov 23
Arsenal 2 Southampton 0 I believe Giroud showed exceptional quality today. The way he haired the ball off Boruc to hair in the first goal was outstanding.

Wenger Knows Best @wengerknowsbest · Nov 24
AVB will be little bit low tonight, after Spurs lost 6-0 at Man City. He did not see that coming. He thought Manuel Pellegrini was an Italian brand of mineral water.

Wenger Knows Best @wengerknowsbest · Nov 24
AVB is still little bit low tonight. He did not see that coming. He thought Sergio Aguero was a war film.

Wenger Knows Best @wengerknowsbest · Nov 25
I feel criticism of Tottenham is little bit harsh. Apart from six goals, indignity and global humiliation, there was not a lot in it.

Wenger Knows Best @wengerknowsbest · Nov 25
Lukas Podolski Two To Three Weeks Away is now only two to three weeks away from being two to three weeks away.

Wenger Knows Best @wengerknowsbest · Nov 26
We want to do well, we want to qualify. We are up for it. We respect Marseille very much, that's why we want to beat them.

Wenger Knows Best @wengerknowsbest · Nov 26
We will not take anything for granted tonight, we have prepared well. Are all of our ducks in a row? No. We don't have any ducks.

November 2013

Wenger Knows Best @wengerknowsbest   Nov 26
Arsenal 2 Marseille 0 We did well. Tonight's result did not threaten to become un-com-fort-able. We had chances to score more, but the win was com-fort-able.

Wenger Knows Best @wengerknowsbest   Nov 26
I feel criticism of Özil's penalty miss is little bit harsh. He is suffering at the moment from little bit cow's-bottom-banjo niggle.

Wenger Knows Best @wengerknowsbest   Nov 27
Overall I prefer my players to maintain club traditions. Should Flamini cut off his sleeves? I don't know, I'm not a tailor.

Wenger Knows Best @wengerknowsbest   Nov 28
Flamini will not cut his sleeves again. Have I had a handbrake fitted to his scissors? I don't want to comment on speculation.

Wenger Knows Best @wengerknowsbest   Nov 29
We look forward now to Cardiff. We have prepared well. Have we washed Szczesny's jersey as little bit precaution? Yes.

Wenger Knows Best @wengerknowsbest   Nov 29
I must say, I did not hear well the chant incident involving Villas Boas. Is he getting slacks in the morning? I don't know.

Wenger Knows Best @wengerknowsbest   Nov 30
Will I sign a new contract as a Christmas present to the medias? I don't know. Chocolates and a firm handshake are usually good enough.

Wenger Knows Best @wengerknowsbest   Nov 30
I believe criticism of Cardiff owner Vincent Tan is little bit harsh. His off-the-shoulder trousers have exceptional quality.

November/December 2013

Wenger Knows Best @wengerknowsbest   Nov 30
Cardiff City 0 Arsenal 3 Ramsey's goals showed exceptional quality. Flamini's goal showed outstanding sleeves. Giroud's hair showed super shine and volume.

Wenger Knows Best @wengerknowsbest   Nov 30
Ramsey is now efficient defensively and efficient offensively. Is he highly defensive? Yes. Is he highly offensive? Well errr, no.

Wenger Knows Best @wengerknowsbest   Nov 30
We are happy yes, but we will not put all our eggs in one basket. Largely because we don't have any baskets. Or, frankly, eggs.

Wenger Knows Best @wengerknowsbest   Dec 1
What happens to our title challenge if Giroud gets injured? I don't know. What happens to it if he doesn't?

Wenger Knows Best @wengerknowsbest   Dec 1
Criticism of Villas Boas is little bit harsh. His results are suffering a small lack of sharpness but he still has exceptional hair.

Wenger Knows Best @wengerknowsbest   Dec 1
I must tell you, for a team that is top of the league despite not having yet played anybody, we are doing exceptionally well.

Wenger Knows Best @wengerknowsbest   Dec 1
Can we win the championship after going the whole season without playing anybody? I don't know. But it's not a bad idea.

Wenger Knows Best @wengerknowsbest   Dec 1
Can we only win the championship if we beat the Chelseas and the Manchester Cities? I don't know. It depends how many there are.

Wenger Knows Best @wengerknowsbest   Dec 2
Is our next game a must-win game? Yes. Every game is a must-win game. Show me a game you must not win.

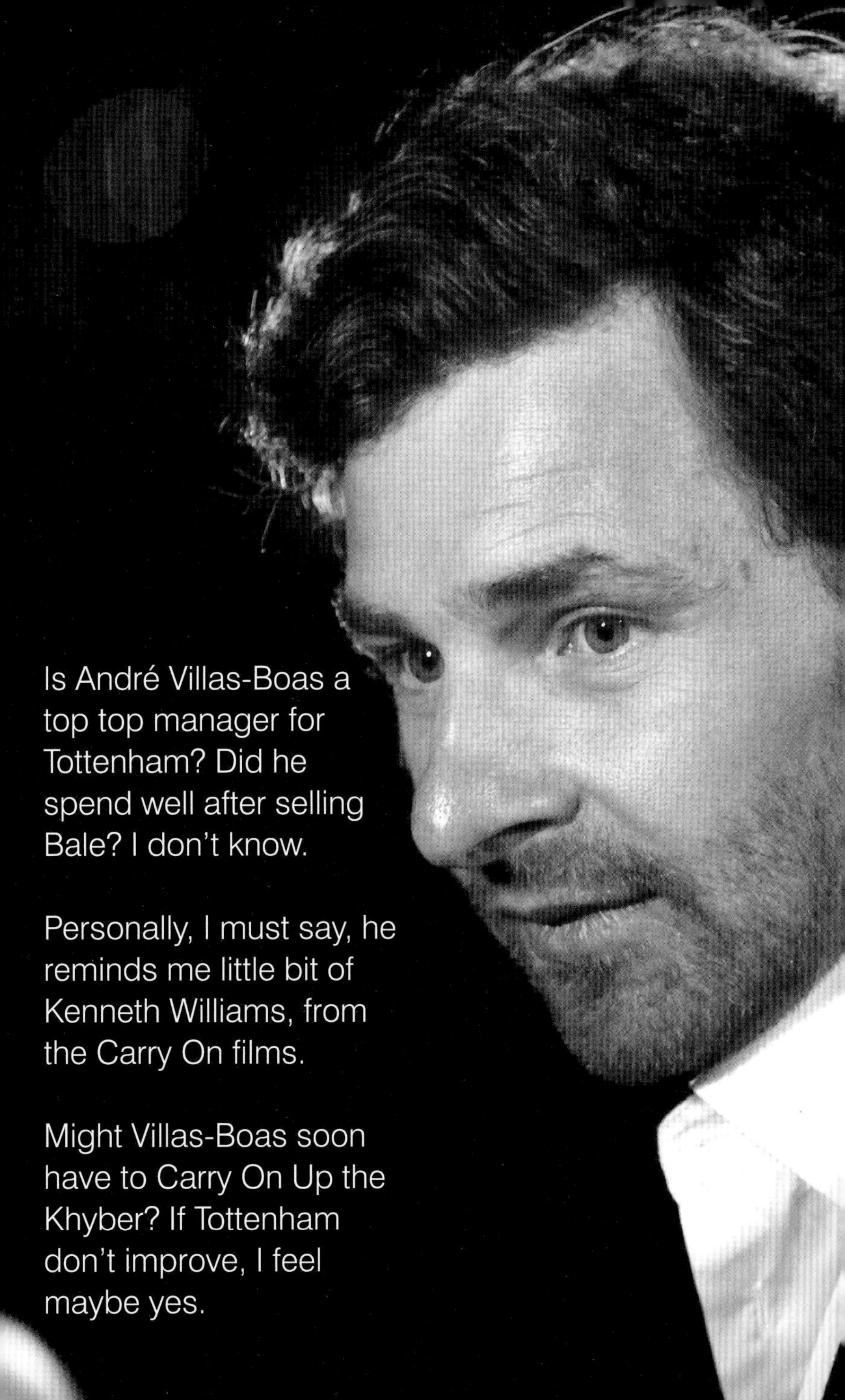Is André Villas-Boas a top top manager for Tottenham? Did he spend well after selling Bale? I don't know.

Personally, I must say, he reminds me little bit of Kenneth Williams, from the Carry On films.

Might Villas-Boas soon have to Carry On Up the Khyber? If Tottenham don't improve, I feel maybe yes.

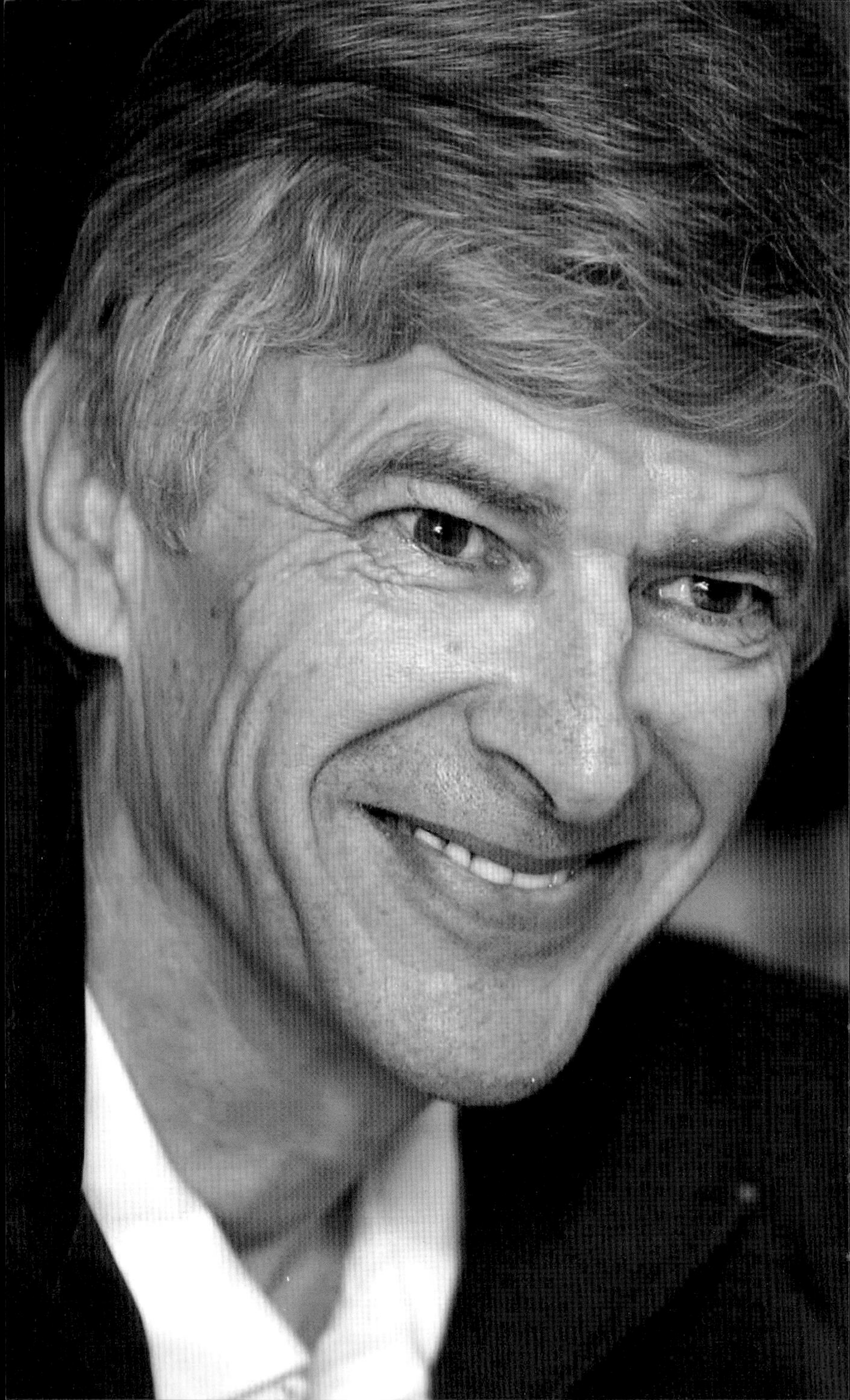

"Arsène? Mauricio Pochettino…"
"……Buenas noches, Mauricio!…"
"Oh Arsène, call me Maurice! It's awfully nice of you to speak in Spanish, but I do speak frightfully good English you know!… "
"…Well errr, you should try little bit English in your post-match interviews!…"
"That would be absolutely splendid old boy, but one must be so careful with that ghastly British press."
"…I must say, Schneiderlin has exceptional quality. Is there maybe little bit small chance we can sign him next summer?…"
"No quiero hacer comentarios sobre la especulación."

I had little bit strange dream last night. I was busy watching Panthrakikos draw 2-2 at Aris Thessaloniki, in the Greek Super League, when the channel changed suddenly and Tomas Rosicky was playing lead guitar in little bit heavy metal funk band.

Did his riffs show exceptional technique? Well no, I must say they lacked little bit sharpness, but I don't like to comment on individual guitarists.

Flamini was on drums, playing little bit like Animal from Sesame Street. Poldi was dancing on stage, thumbing to the music and smiling. Was he little bit like Bez, from the Happy Mondays? I don't know Bez.

Per Mertesacker was the lead vocalist and I must say he led the group with fantastic spirit and exceptional musical potential. He played slap bass funky punk of outstanding quality.

What does this dream mean? I don't know. But at least now I know why our fans call Mertesacker a Big Funky German.

"Big Funky German! We got a Big Funky German! Big Funky Gerrrrrman......"

December 2013

Wenger Knows Best
@wengerknowsbest

Well I must say, I am little bit jaded after a few small sherries. Chestnuts roasting on an open fire? No, they're fine thank you.

25/12/2013

December 2013

Wenger Knows Best @wengerknowsbest — Dec 2
Have we failed with a £6.5m bid for Pato? No. There is a small lunch-transfer niggle. I merely asked Gazidis to get me some paté.

Wenger Knows Best @wengerknowsbest — Dec 2
Is Benteke suffering little bit form niggle? Yes. Is it part of a plan to drop his price in time for January? I don't know about that.

Wenger Knows Best @wengerknowsbest — Dec 3
Lukas Podolski Two To Three Weeks Away is now sadly two to three more weeks away from being two to three weeks away.

Wenger Knows Best @wengerknowsbest — Dec 3
Podolski has had a small setback. His hamstring is alright, but he has aggravated little bit smile-double-thumbs-up niggle.

Wenger Knows Best @wengerknowsbest — Dec 3
Does Alvaro Morata have super potential? Yes. Has he signed on a six-month loan deal? I don't know Morata.

Wenger Knows Best @wengerknowsbest — Dec 3
Jenko in, Sagna out. In out in out, shake it all about. Little bit hamstring niggle and you turn around, that's what it's all about.

Wenger Knows Best @wengerknowsbest — Dec 3
Am I worried about the safety of flares at matches? Yes. I remember little bit zip niggle I had with a purple pair in 1976.

Wenger Knows Best @wengerknowsbest — Dec 3
Overall, travel to the Hull game should be more com-fort-able now that the little bit Piccadilly Line niggle has been called off.

December 2013

Wenger Knows Best @wengerknowsbest   Dec 4
You say Mor-ata, I say Mor-arta, let's call the whole thing off?
I don't want to comment on speculation.

Wenger Knows Best @wengerknowsbest   Dec 4
Might I rest Giroud against Hull? Yes. Is the big fella ready to
play instead and we put it in little bit mixer? Yes, Gunnersaurus
is up for it.

Wenger Knows Best @wengerknowsbest   Dec 4
Does Steve Bruce look like Mrs Doubtfire? Well errr, I feel that
is little bit harsh. Then again, I don't know Doubtfire.

Wenger Knows Best @wengerknowsbest   Dec 4
Arsenal 2 Hull City 0 We are happy tonight. We had enough
petrol and the gearbox and fan belt were exceptional. I must
say, Bendtner's hair did well.

Wenger Knows Best @wengerknowsbest   Dec 4
We showed efficiently efficient efficiency and consistently
consistent consistency. We looked the Tigers in the eye and
were survivors.

Wenger Knows Best @wengerknowsbest   Dec 5
Moyes will be little bit low today after losing to Everton. He
did not see that coming. He thought the real Oviedo was a
football club in northern Spain.

Wenger Knows Best @wengerknowsbest   Dec 5
Is it right for Moyes to be under pressure already for his job at
United? No. I hope he is there for as long as possible.

Wenger Knows Best @wengerknowsbest   Dec 5
Did I watch Match Of The Day? Yes. Did I hear Fowler say we
can win the championship? Yes. Did I hear Shearer say we
can't? I don't know Shearer.

December 2013

Wenger Knows Best @wengerknowsbest · Dec 5
Is Gary Lineker right to give the impression we can win the championship? I don't know. But I prefer it to his last impression of me.

Wenger Knows Best @wengerknowsbest · Dec 5
Do we regret not offering more than £40,000,001 for Suarez? Yes. Will we try again? Yes, but I don't want to comment on speculation.

Wenger Knows Best @wengerknowsbest · Dec 5
"Yes not bad thank you. Now where were we, Mr Ayre?...... Oh yes, £48,575,621?..." "No." "£48,575,622?..." "No." "£48,575,623?..."

Wenger Knows Best @wengerknowsbest · Dec 5
I feel Josh Kroenke can bring outstanding quality to this club as a non-executive director. Can he also fill in as back-up to Giroud? Well, no.

Wenger Knows Best @wengerknowsbest · Dec 5
I believe Josh Kroenke can bring exceptional character, a fantastic attitude and his own hair.

Wenger Knows Best @wengerknowsbest · Dec 5
"£49,999,998?..." "No." "£49,999,999?..." "No." "£50,000,000?..." "No." "NO!?!..." "No." "...£50,000,001?" "No." "NO!?!......£50,000,002..."

Wenger Knows Best @wengerknowsbest · Dec 6
"£52,431,691..?" "No." "£52,431,692..?" "No." "£52,431,693..?" "No." "£52,431,694..?" "No." "£52,431,695..?" "No." "£52,431,696..?" "No."

Wenger Knows Best @wengerknowsbest · Dec 6
"£52,431,697..?" "No." "£52,431,698..?" "No." "£52,431,699..?" "No." "Can we have little bit break, I have a press conference now?" "Sure."

December 2013

Wenger Knows Best @wengerknowsbest · Dec 6
Sagna is out against Everton this weekend. His hair is close to a return, but his hamstring still has little bit niggle.

Wenger Knows Best @wengerknowsbest · Dec 6
Little bit World Cup group G niggle for Germany. Joachim will be little bit Löw tonight. That's it.

Wenger Knows Best @wengerknowsbest · Dec 6
Hodgson will be little bit low tonight. He did not see that coming. He thought Costa Rica was a nice cup of coffee.

Wenger Knows Best @wengerknowsbest · Dec 6
Hodgson is still little bit low tonight. He did not see that coming. He thought Belo Horizonte might be an exotic dance act.

Wenger Knows Best @wengerknowsbest · Dec 7
I feel criticism of the England cricket team is little bit harsh. Apart from the batting, bowling and fielding, there is not a lot in it.

Wenger Knows Best @wengerknowsbest · Dec 7
Has England suffered little bit from small Ashes niggles with their handbrake, petrol tank and fan belt? I don't know. I'm not a mechanic.

Wenger Knows Best @wengerknowsbest · Dec 8
I did not see yesterday's incidents, we were preparing for Everton. We are up for it. We don't want little bit sticky Toffees pudding.

Wenger Knows Best @wengerknowsbest · Dec 8
Is still too early to talk about winning the championship? Yes. Of course. It is only 8am.

December 2013

Wenger Knows Best @wengerknowsbest   Dec 8
Arsenal 1 Everton 1 Szczesny is little bit low right now. He did not see that coming. He thought Gerard Deulofeu was the French actor in Green Card.

Wenger Knows Best @wengerknowsbest   Dec 9
Is spot-fixing rife? Yes, I believe Clearasil has consistently shown top quality at tackling little bit acne niggle.

Wenger Knows Best @wengerknowsbest   Dec 10
We fly today to Naples. We want to do well. We want to qualify. We also want little bit Nutella ice cream, it has exceptional quality.

Wenger Knows Best @wengerknowsbest   Dec 10
Bouldy wants little bit Tuesday Club tonight in Naples, he is up for it. I must say, I do like limoncello, but I can't manage 8 pints.

Wenger Knows Best @wengerknowsbest   Dec 11
Is this club similar to the volcano nearby, Vesuvias? Yes. We are both little bit dormant, but once we start there will be no stopping us.

Wenger Knows Best @wengerknowsbest   Dec 11
Napoli 2 Arsenal 0 I feel criticism of Arteta is little bit harsh. His hair started very well but dropped maybe little bit physically in the second half.

Wenger Knows Best @wengerknowsbest   Dec 11
I must tell you, Giroud was carrying a small gearbox niggle coming into tonight's game. He might have to go in for little bit MOT.

Wenger Knows Best @wengerknowsbest   Dec 12
Higua-in Higua-out, in out in out shake it all about. Little bit injustice but you turn around, that's what it's all about.

December 2013

Wenger Knows Best @wengerknowsbest · Dec 12

We will prepare well for City. We will be up for it. They have achieved great success since they were formed five years ago.

Wenger Knows Best @wengerknowsbest · Dec 12

Can the England cricket team recover from little bit form niggle? Yes. But they dropped little bit physically in the Second Test.

Wenger Knows Best @wengerknowsbest · Dec 13

Do we want to play at City on Saturday morning after playing in Italy on Wednesday night? No. But I don't want to complain about fixtures.

Wenger Knows Best @wengerknowsbest · Dec 13

Sagna needs a small test, for City. Podolski is alright, but might be little bit short. Cazorla is little bit short.

Wenger Knows Best @wengerknowsbest · Dec 13

Will we give Cazorla little bit birthday cake today? Yes, of course. Grilled chicken and broccoli? I hope so, yes.

Wenger Knows Best @wengerknowsbest · Dec 13

Is van Persie still an Arsenal man at heart? I feel yes. Is he still an Arsenal man at thigh? I don't want to comment on football reasons.

Wenger Knows Best @wengerknowsbest · Dec 14

Manchester City 6 Arsenal 3 We lacked today maybe little bit fuel injection. Some small handbrake turns caused a suspension niggle. Plus we conceded six goals.

Wenger Knows Best @wengerknowsbest · Dec 14

I believe 6-3 today was little bit harsh. I feel 6-4 or 6-5 would be closer, or maybe 6-6 and we take the match to a tie-break.

December 2013

Wenger Knows Best @wengerknowsbest   Dec 14
We are still little bit low tonight. We did not see that coming.
I thought Rio Fernandinho still played for Man United.

Wenger Knows Best @wengerknowsbest   Dec 14
On reflection, I feel that our surprise tactic to drop little
bit physically from the beginning of the first half did not
really work.

Wenger Knows Best @wengerknowsbest   Dec 15
Did Wilshere make a gesture to the City fans? I don't know.
I did not see the incident. He might be carrying little bit
finger niggle.

Wenger Knows Best @wengerknowsbest   Dec 15
I did not completely hear the crowd speculation incident at
Tottenham, but yes maybe Villas Boas will be getting slacks in
the morning.

Wenger Knows Best @wengerknowsbest   Dec 16
We don't mind who we get in the Champions League draw.
As long as we avoid Real Madrid, Atletico Madrid, Barcelona,
Bayern Munich & PSG.

Wenger Knows Best @wengerknowsbest   Dec 16
Our Champions League draw is exceptionally difficult. But with
outstanding technical quality, Bayern Munich might still have a
small chance.

Wenger Knows Best @wengerknowsbest   Dec 16
I must tell you, we take no pleasure in Villas Boas being
sacked. Is he now in a negative spiral? I don't want to
comment on speculation.

Wenger Knows Best @wengerknowsbest   Dec 16
Another one bites the dust at Tottenham. Villa Boas had one
vision but it is hard being under pressure. Sometimes even I
want to break free.

December 2013

Wenger Knows Best @wengerknowsbest · Dec 16
Were Tottenham little bit stone cold crazy to sack Villas Boas? I believe yes. Was he waiting for the hammer to fall? I don't know.

Wenger Knows Best @wengerknowsbest · Dec 16
I hear Villas Boas is in little bit frame for an exceptional role at Sparta Prague or Slavia Prague. Bohemian Rhapsody? Yes.

Wenger Knows Best @wengerknowsbest · Dec 16
We do not want to rain on Tottenham's parade. Might today be good timing to announce my new contract? Yes, why not?

Wenger Knows Best @wengerknowsbest · Dec 16
We will be up for it against Chelsea. We will show solidarity. The 1980's shipworkers' union from Poland? Not that sort of solidarity.

Wenger Knows Best @wengerknowsbest · Dec 16
"...£57,847,361..?" "No." "£57,847,362..?" "No." "£57,847,363..?" "No." "£57,847,364..?" "No." "£57,847,365..?" "No." "£57,847,366..?" "No."

Wenger Knows Best @wengerknowsbest · Dec 16
"You do know Suarez is at our stadium tonight. For little bit awards? We could keep him there..." "Eh? Do one!" "Hmmm...£57,847,491.." "No."

Wenger Knows Best @wengerknowsbest · Dec 17
Is Sagna locked in contract negotiations? Yes. Will we let him out if he doesn't sign one? I don't know.

Wenger Knows Best @wengerknowsbest · Dec 18
We are delighted to release legends documentaries for Henry, Bergkamp, Winterburn and Keown. When is the Almunia one released? I don't know.

December 2013

Wenger Knows Best @wengerknowsbest — Dec 18
Am I little bit bitter about the Capital One Cup, after losing to Bradford and recently Chelsea? No. I don't know the Capital One Cup.

Wenger Knows Best @wengerknowsbest — Dec 18
There is little bit un-com-fort-able transfer confusion tonight. I merely told Gazidis that I respect the work of Willem Dafoe.

Wenger Knows Best @wengerknowsbest — Dec 18
"Hello, Sherwood? Yes, very good! No, I don't think anybody suspects a thing. Playing Adebayor was an exceptional touch, very funny!"

Wenger Knows Best @wengerknowsbest — Dec 19
Is Suarez's agent having discussions over a new Liverpool deal, which would end any negotiations to sign him? I don't know Suarez's agent.

Wenger Knows Best @wengerknowsbest — Dec 19
"Morning Ian. Yes, not bad. Where were we? £59,131,475..?" "No." "£59,131,476..?" "No." "£59,131,477..?" "No." "£59,131,478..?" "No.."

Wenger Knows Best @wengerknowsbest — Dec 19
I feel a two-game ban for Wilshere, for raising one finger, is little bit harsh. It's a good thing he didn't raise more fingers.

Wenger Knows Best @wengerknowsbest — Dec 19
Should Wilshere have raised a finger to City fans? No. He should have raised four fingers and a thumb. There is no ban for waving.

Wenger Knows Best @wengerknowsbest — Dec 19
Does Wilshere have little bit involuntary-finger-raising-spasm-niggle? I don't know. But as an appeal it is worth a try.

December 2013

Wenger Knows Best @wengerknowsbest · Dec 19
I must say, our fancy dress Christmas party was outstanding. Did I go dressed as little bit zip niggle? No.

Wenger Knows Best @wengerknowsbest · Dec 19
Have I written to Santa to ask for an extra special present next year? No. Tottenham are already the gift that keeps giving.

Wenger Knows Best @wengerknowsbest · Dec 19
Might Giroud get a two-match ban for putting up a finger after our Christmas party? No. He was merely adjusting little bit sleeve niggle.

Wenger Knows Best @wengerknowsbest · Dec 19
When I said earlier that "Tottenham are the gift that keeps giving" it was of course only little bit Christmas banter. They did send a card.

Wenger Knows Best @wengerknowsbest · Dec 19
Did Villas Boas write in the Tottenham Christmas card? Yes. Something about a "spiral" and "May". Nevermind. Small sacking niggle.

Wenger Knows Best @wengerknowsbest · Dec 20
Is Vincent Tan fit and proper to own a football club? Are off-the-shoulder trousers a good look? I don't know.

Wenger Knows Best @wengerknowsbest · Dec 20
Podolski in, Koscielny out. In out in out, shake it all about. You try not to lose 6-3 and you turn around, that's what it's all about.

Wenger Knows Best @wengerknowsbest · Dec 20
Why am I still in this job? I don't know. There is no real secret. I just haven't been sacked yet.

December 2013

Wenger Knows Best @wengerknowsbest　Dec 20
Do I expect to be busy in the January transfer window? At the moment, no. How about now? No. And now? No. Now? Maybe little bit.

Wenger Knows Best @wengerknowsbest　Dec 20
Does Luis Suarez's new Liverpool contract have a clear release clause? Maybe yes. Is it more than £40,000,001? Probably.

Wenger Knows Best @wengerknowsbest　Dec 21
Is Tim Sherwood an Arsenal supporter? I believe yes. Is he a good choice as little bit permanent new Tottenham manager. I believe yes.

Wenger Knows Best @wengerknowsbest　Dec 21
Are we still top of the league? No. But it is too early to talk about Liverpool winning the championship.

Wenger Knows Best @wengerknowsbest　Dec 21
"Evening Ian." "Arsène? He's signed a new contract!" "£63,548,712?" "Look, he's just not for sale." "..........£63,548,713......"

Wenger Knows Best @wengerknowsbest　Dec 22
I believe UEFA should now ban away goals. Especially when other teams score them against us.

Wenger Knows Best @wengerknowsbest　Dec 23
Is it true that I have never beaten Mourinho? No. I must tell you, he is exceptionally poor at Scrabble.

Wenger Knows Best @wengerknowsbest　Dec 23
We have listened to all advice and prepared well for tonight's terrible storm but, I must tell you, we have played Chelsea before.

December 2013

Wenger Knows Best @wengerknowsbest · Dec 23
Arteta and Giroud are currently having late fitness tests. Given tonight's severe weather, both are at risk of major hair niggle.

Wenger Knows Best @wengerknowsbest · Dec 23
Arsenal 0 Chelsea 0 We are of course little bit disappointed to draw 0-0, but on the other hand it is 6-3 better than losing 6-3.

Wenger Knows Best @wengerknowsbest · Dec 24
"Sherwood? Afternoon. Yes, you got an extra year out of Levy! It should give us enough time for little bit Operation Decay From Within…"

Wenger Knows Best @wengerknowsbest · Dec 24
I must tell you, I had little bit strange dream last night. Mike Dean was starring in a new film, "Referee Without A Cause".

Wenger Knows Best @wengerknowsbest · Dec 24
There has been little bit confusion over what to leave out for Santa. Gazidis is currently out buying a meat pie and a parrot.

Wenger Knows Best @wengerknowsbest · Dec 24
After a small Christmas confusion with the Spanish transfer market, Gazidis is now planning an early swoop for Feliz Navidad.

Wenger Knows Best @wengerknowsbest · Dec 25
I would like to wish everybody a Christmas of outstanding quality, super spirit and exceptional hair.

Wenger Knows Best @wengerknowsbest · Dec 25
To everybody spending more time today with their families than usual, I wish you all exceptional mental strength.

December 2013

 **Wenger Knows Best** @wengerknowsbest · Dec 25
Well I must say, I am super super stuffed now. I feel I may
have overdone it little bit on the grilled turkey and broccoli.

 **Wenger Knows Best** @wengerknowsbest · Dec 25
Well I must say, I am little bit jaded after a few small sherries.
Chestnuts roasting on an open fire? No, they're fine thank you.

 **Wenger Knows Best** @wengerknowsbest · Dec 25
Having had a few sherries, I have written little bit new Arsenal
lyrics to some Christmas carols. Will I share them? Yes,
why not?

 **Wenger Knows Best** @wengerknowsbest · Dec 25
Away in a manager, Niall Quinn for a bed, Lit-tle Nelson Vivas,
Lay down his sweet head...

 **Wenger Knows Best** @wengerknowsbest · Dec 25
...Seb Svard in Ian Wright's sky, Looked Danny O'Shea, Lit-tle
Nelson Vivas, asleep on Martin Hayes.

 **Wenger Knows Best** @wengerknowsbest · Dec 25
Do my new Arsenal Christmas carols so far have top top
quality? I don't know. Will I carry on with the rest of them?
Yes.

 **Wenger Knows Best** @wengerknowsbest · Dec 25
Good King Wenger last looked out, on the feast of Sweden.
Freddie Ljungberg ate pizza, deep pan crisp and even.

 **Wenger Knows Best** @wengerknowsbest · Dec 25
Deck John Halls with boughs of holly. Fa la little bit, la la la la.
Remi Garde and Gilles Grimandi. Fa la little bit, la la la la.

December 2013

Wenger Knows Best @wengerknowsbest · Dec 25
Good King Henry last looked out, on something elementary. It had super quality, his iTunes documentary.

Wenger Knows Best @wengerknowsbest · Dec 26
We look forward to West Ham today. We are up for it, but I Adam and Eve they are in little bit right two and eight.

Wenger Knows Best @wengerknowsbest · Dec 26
Is Mourinho still a "special one"? No. I think of him more as little bit pantomime villain. Is he behind me? Yes. By two points.

Wenger Knows Best @wengerknowsbest · Dec 26
Cazorla in, Rosicky out. In out in out, shake it all about. Not yet resting Özil and you turn around. That's what it's all about.

Wenger Knows Best @wengerknowsbest · Dec 26
West Ham 1 Arsenal 3 Allardyce will be little bit low tonight. He did not see that coming. He thought he was still good enough to coach Real Madrid.

Wenger Knows Best @wengerknowsbest · Dec 26
Allardyce believes he would be taken more seriously if he was foreign. Might some say his football is foreign already? I don't know.

Wenger Knows Best @wengerknowsbest · Dec 27
I remain absolutely convinced we have not over-worked Ramsey. Will he rest today? Yes. After he finishes mowing the pitch.

Wenger Knows Best @wengerknowsbest · Dec 27
I believe criticism of Vincent Tan is little bit harsh. He might not have worked half a day in football but he was fantastic in Goldfinger.

December 2013

 **Wenger Knows Best** @wengerknowsbest · Dec 28
We are up for it against Newcastle, preparations are going
well. Have we put in a bid yet for Cabaye? No.

 **Wenger Knows Best** @wengerknowsbest · Dec 28
I must say, the locals in Newcastle have given us a very warm
welcome. Many waved at us as we arrived. At least I think it
was waving.

 **Wenger Knows Best** @wengerknowsbest · Dec 28
Do Newcastle fans love their football? Yes, but I believe
they lack little bit knowledge about our players. I don't know
Wayne Kerr.

 **Wenger Knows Best** @wengerknowsbest · Dec 29
Newcastle 0 Arsenal 1 We showed today outstanding
defensive solidity and exceptional mental strength. Especially
Giroud's hair, for quiffing the winner.

 **Wenger Knows Best** @wengerknowsbest · Dec 29
Well yes, we are delighted to be top of the championship
half-way, but I feel it is still too early to talk about
the championship.

 **Wenger Knows Best** @wengerknowsbest · Dec 29
Did Cabaye play well? Yes. Is he powerful? Yes. Is there
no greater power, than the power of Cabaye? I don't
know Madonna.

 **Wenger Knows Best** @wengerknowsbest · Dec 30
There is little bit confusion over Balotelli. I merely mentioned to
Gazidis that I believe Halle Berry has exceptional quality.

 **Wenger Knows Best** @wengerknowsbest · Dec 30
Halle Berry has an Academy award, exceptional hair and is
not cup-tied in Europe. But it's hard to sign players in January.

December 2013

 **Wenger Knows Best** @wengerknowsbest — Dec 31
I must tell you, I believe you do not need to wait until a New Year to make resolutions. But I don't want to comment on celebrations.

 **Wenger Knows Best** @wengerknowsbest — Dec 31
Podolski in, Ozil out, Ramsey out, Giroud out, Gibbo out, Kallis out, Tendulkar out, England cricket team out, 2013 almost out.

 **Wenger Knows Best** @wengerknowsbest — Dec 31
In 2013 we have shown consistently consistent consistency. In 2014 we hope to show silveristically silver silverware.

 **Wenger Knows Best** @wengerknowsbest — Dec 31
We are on alert for transfers. If any lerts of top quality become available we will do it.

 **Wenger Knows Best** @wengerknowsbest — Dec 31
Will Giroud's injury make us need to sign a replacement? I don't know. It is hard to find quality hair in January.

 **Wenger Knows Best** @wengerknowsbest — Dec 31
We have trained well for Cardiff, we are up for it. Footballistically we are little bit short. Is Cazorla short? No he is 5ft 6 actually.

 **Wenger Knows Best** @wengerknowsbest — Dec 31
I remain absolutely convinced my players will rest well tonight, don't worry. Does Bouldy have little bit plans for me? I believe yes.

 **Wenger Knows Best** @wengerknowsbest — Dec 31
What does Bouldy have in store, to celebrate the New Year? I don't know. But he did mention something about a 'Tuesday Club special'.

"You have exceptional quality Thierry!"

"Yes boss!"

"Do you fancy facing Spurs soon?"

"Yes boss!"

"Are you any good at fixing little bit zip niggle?"

"I don't know boss."

"Arsène? Tim Sherwood..."

"......Evening Tim. Looking forward to our game soon!?!..."

"Yes mate! I'd be telling porkies if I said I wasn't!"

"I must say, you are doing well at Tottenham. Maybe little bit too well! Has anybody seen your Arsenal tattoo yet?"

"I don't know boss, I don't want to comment on speculation. Ha ha! Seriously gaffer, I'd love to be part of your coaching staff next season, if Spurs let me go in the summer."

" Well err, we let you know."

I can now reveal exclusively for the first time
the inside story of how Emmanuel Adebayor
joined Manchester City for £25m.

Adebayor had super potential, fantastic spirit and
exceptional hair. We knew that, but he lacked
maybe little bit consistently consistent consistency.

City wanted to finish above us in the championship
and felt they could do that by signing two of our
most exceptional players. Thankfully, they chose
Adebayor and Kolo Touré.

We accepted a fee of £15 for Kolo. We were happy
with that. City faxed back to apologise that they
had missed a small small 'm' from the fee. So we
felt obliged to accept £15m for Kolo, which was
little bit un-com-fort-able.

For Adebayor, negotiations to reach £25m were
much simpler. City offered us £50m. We said "You
can have him for nothing". So they agreed to meet
us half-way.

January 2014

Wenger Knows Best
@wengerknowsbest

Arsenal 2 Tottenham 0 Did Walcott make a gesture at Tottenham fans? Yes. I believe they asked which mobile phone operator he uses and he gestured '@O2'.

04/01/2014

January 2014

Wenger Knows Best @wengerknowsbest　　　　Jan 1
"Gazidis?...You've signed two players already? That's exceptional - hang on little bit. It's Happy New Year, not April Fools' Day..."

Wenger Knows Best @wengerknowsbest　　　　Jan 1
Well I must wish you all a very Happy New Year. Can we win the championship this season? Yes. But please don't tell anybody.

Wenger Knows Best @wengerknowsbest　　　　Jan 1
I can assure you, we are already working day and night to add super-exceptional quality to this squad. Are we close to signing anybody? No.

Wenger Knows Best @wengerknowsbest　　　　Jan 1
Arsenal 2 Cardiff City 0 We showed today resiliently resilient resilience. Cardiff dropped little bit physically in the second half, so we released the handbrake.

Wenger Knows Best @wengerknowsbest　　　　Jan 1
Podolski lacked today maybe little bit sharpness. And pace. And maybe finishing. Apart from that, he played quite well.

Wenger Knows Best @wengerknowsbest　　　　Jan 1
Happy New Year? Yes, we did well to beat Cardiff in difficult conditions, but it is little bit early to talk about the New Year.

Wenger Knows Best @wengerknowsbest　　　　Jan 2
Have I had breakfast yet? I don't know. But if I can find food of exceptional quality I will do it.

Wenger Knows Best @wengerknowsbest　　　　Jan 2
Why did I wear tracksuit and trainers against Cardiff? Why not? Was it little bit bet with Pulis? No. Do I have to wear a baseball cap? No.

January 2014

Wenger Knows Best @wengerknowsbest — Jan 2
We are little bit short on strikers but we should be okay for Tottenham. Walcott, Podolski, Akpom, Gnabry, Merson, Henry and Henry's statue.

Wenger Knows Best @wengerknowsbest — Jan 2
Is Bergkamp's statue ready? Yes. Could it be made available for Saturday? Yes. But it lacks maybe little bit sharpness.

Wenger Knows Best @wengerknowsbest — Jan 2
If Arshavin had a statue that could be available for Tottenham, might it be little bit short? Yes.

Wenger Knows Best @wengerknowsbest — Jan 2
"Hello Ian, happy new year." "Hiya Arsène, he's still not for sale though. At any price." "£86,000,001. Final offer."

Wenger Knows Best @wengerknowsbest — Jan 3
Berbatov is not a name I have considered at the moment. How about now? No. And now? No. Now? No. But now you mention it.

Wenger Knows Best @wengerknowsbest — Jan 3
Is Berbatov a smokescreen? I don't know. Is he a smokescreen for the smokescreen? No. A smokescreen for the smokescreen's smokescreen? No.

Wenger Knows Best @wengerknowsbest — Jan 3
"Sherwood? Yes, well done. Although you are doing little bit too well! Don't be too convincing! Adebayor red card niggle again? Why not?"

Wenger Knows Best @wengerknowsbest — Jan 3
Did I enjoy lunch? I don't want to talk about that. Lunch is not a meal we have considered at the moment.

January 2014

Wenger Knows Best @wengerknowsbest — Jan 4
"Sherwood? Afternoon. Yes, should be fun. Can you wear your Arsenal top under your Tottenham outfit? Maybe little bit unwise."

Wenger Knows Best @wengerknowsbest — Jan 4
Arsenal 2 Tottenham 0 Did Walcott make a gesture at Tottenham fans? Yes. I believe they asked which mobile phone operator he uses and he gestured '@O2'.

Wenger Knows Best @wengerknowsbest — Jan 4
Did Tottenham fans throw a lot of money at Walcott? Yes. But what is a few more quid after £100m?

Wenger Knows Best @wengerknowsbest — Jan 4
"Sherwood? Good evening! Yes, I enjoyed it too! Well done. Sorry? Can you now have Brady's job in the Academy? We let you know."

Wenger Knows Best @wengerknowsbest — Jan 5
Did we enjoy beating Tottenham again? Yes, of course. But it is too early to talk about a power shift.

Wenger Knows Best @wengerknowsbest — Jan 5
I feel criticism of David Moyes is little bit harsh. He is just suffering from little bit 'not Alex Ferguson' niggle.

Wenger Knows Best @wengerknowsbest — Jan 5
"Boss?" "...Yes." "It's me...Robin." "Right." "I want to come back." "Sorry, I didn't catch that." "I didn't mean it." "No, can't hear you."

Wenger Knows Best @wengerknowsbest — Jan 5
"Boss. It's me, Robin." "Yes, we had little bit reception niggle!" "Please take me back!" "...I don't know. What does your little boy say?"

January 2014

 **Wenger Knows Best** @wengerknowsbest — Jan 5
"Ivan? Evening. Yes, United out of the FA Cup, little bit funny! Do I know Rooney's release clause? I don't know. Think of a number and start adding ones."

 **Wenger Knows Best** @wengerknowsbest — Jan 6
We will respect Coventry. Micky Quinn and Peter Ndlovu have caused us little bit problems before, so we will be up for it.

 **Wenger Knows Best** @wengerknowsbest — Jan 6
We are pleased Walcott has not been punished for his scoreline gesture. Teaching basic maths is an important part of our community work.

 **Wenger Knows Best** @wengerknowsbest — Jan 6
I must tell you, Theo's niggle will not ruin our season. We will show outstanding resilience, top quality and exceptional mental strength.

 **Wenger Knows Best** @wengerknowsbest — Jan 7
Does Theo's injury force us now to dip little bit into a transfer war chest? I don't know. We are not at war.

 **Wenger Knows Best** @wengerknowsbest — Jan 7
Theo's injury is exceptionally un-com-fort-able. Overall I feel he is a victim of little bit inconsistently inconsistent inconsistency.

 **Wenger Knows Best** @wengerknowsbest — Jan 7
I can assure you, we have been today very very active in the market. Chapel Market, up The Angel. Little bit fruit and veg.

 **Wenger Knows Best** @wengerknowsbest — Jan 8
We have been busy day and night, night and day, looking for players of top top quality. Have we found any? I'm not telling you.

January 2014

Wenger Knows Best @wengerknowsbest — Jan 8
Might we soon be able to play that striker we signed back in the summer? Sanogo? No, it is perfectly possible.

Wenger Knows Best @wengerknowsbest — Jan 9
Undisclosed in undisclosed out, in out in out shake it all about. You loan out Chuba Akpom and you turn around, that's what it's all about.

Wenger Knows Best @wengerknowsbest — Jan 9
Akpom Akpom, Chuba Akpom. He can show top quality at Brentford now on loan. Akpom Akpom, Chuba Akpom, maybe he can turn The Bees on?

Wenger Knows Best @wengerknowsbest — Jan 10
Do I like the January transfer window? No. I don't like January. I don't like transfers. And I don't like windows.

Wenger Knows Best @wengerknowsbest — Jan 10
I must tell you, I believe @Podolski10 is one of the best finishers I have ever seen. Even better than Gervinho? Yes.

Wenger Knows Best @wengerknowsbest — Jan 10
Will we sign somebody to cover little bit for Theo, or wait till the summer? I don't want to Julian Draxler comment on speculation.

Wenger Knows Best @wengerknowsbest — Jan 11
Has Chelsea's goalkeeper ever conceded a goal against Hull City? I don't know. I'd Petr Cech.

Wenger Knows Best @wengerknowsbest — Jan 12
Do Chelsea's reserve goalkeepers have an exceptional sense of humour? Yes. I believe one of them is Hilario.

January 2014

Wenger Knows Best @wengerknowsbest · Jan 13
We are especially up for it tonight against Villa. We want to respond after suffering maybe little bit blip on the opening day.

Wenger Knows Best @wengerknowsbest · Jan 13
I believe Gnabry has everything in his game. He has a lot in his locker. Boots, shin-pads, gloves, spare gloves and little bit hair trimmer.

Wenger Knows Best @wengerknowsbest · Jan 13
Is tonight's game at Villa a must-win? Yes. Of course. But show me a game you must not win.

Wenger Knows Best @wengerknowsbest · Jan 13
Has Pardew ever suffered little bit heat-of-the-moment niggle and insulted me, like he did Pellegrini? I don't know Pardew.

Wenger Knows Best @wengerknowsbest · Jan 13
Aston Villa 1 Arsenal 2 Well errr, that was little bit close. We started well but the handbrake's gearbox dropped maybe little bit physically in the second half.

Wenger Knows Best @wengerknowsbest · Jan 13
Rosicky has maybe a broken nose. Monreal has a small chance of a broken metatarsal. And my coat has recurrence of little bit zip niggle.

Wenger Knows Best @wengerknowsbest · Jan 13
Was Pardew abusive to me once at Upton Park? Yes, little bit. Did I respond? No. I believe soon after he was sacked.

Wenger Knows Best @wengerknowsbest · Jan 14
My coat injury might be more serious than little bit zip niggle. We will know more after the scan. Is it out for the season? I don't know.

January 2014

Wenger Knows Best @wengerknowsbest — Jan 14
If my little bit zip niggle is worse than first feared might we bring in a new coat? Yes. If I can find exceptional quality I will do it.

Wenger Knows Best @wengerknowsbest — Jan 15
I must tell you, there is little bit confusion over races for Draxler. I merely told Gazidis I quite like dragster races.

Wenger Knows Best @wengerknowsbest — Jan 15
Could our German players help us little bit to sign Draxler? Yes. Of course. But I don't like to talk about individual names.

Wenger Knows Best @wengerknowsbest — Jan 15
I can assure you, we do our business in private. We respect everybody. If there is any news on Draxler you will be the first to know.

Wenger Knows Best @wengerknowsbest — Jan 15
Rosicky has little bit nose niggle, but his hair looks to be alright.

Wenger Knows Best @wengerknowsbest — Jan 15
Is Chelsea's new signing Nemanja Matic? Yes. Is he systematic? Is he hydromatic? Is he ultramatic? I don't know Grease.

Wenger Knows Best @wengerknowsbest — Jan 16
I can tell you, we are now very very close to a new striker. We play Fulham on Saturday and they only signed Clint Dempsey the other week.

Wenger Knows Best @wengerknowsbest — Jan 16
Have we agreed a deal to sign Paul-Georges Ntep from Auxerre? I don't know. I don't want to comment on Nspeculation.

January 2014

Wenger Knows Best @wengerknowsbest · Jan 16
The Oscar nominations have top quality but, I must say,
I was little bit surprised Januzaj was not nominated for
'Sunderland Away'.

Wenger Knows Best @wengerknowsbest · Jan 17
Will Rosicky wear a face mask against Fulham? Yes. Greek
yoghurt, olive oil and with cucumbers over his eyes? Not that
sort of face mask.

Wenger Knows Best @wengerknowsbest · Jan 17
I believe Rosicky is exceptionally versatile. He can play in the
middle, down the flanks, or as the lead role in Phantom of
the Opera.

Wenger Knows Best @wengerknowsbest · Jan 17
What is Gnabry's ideal position? What position will he end
up? I don't know. I don't want to comment on speculation. But
hopefully 1st.

Wenger Knows Best @wengerknowsbest · Jan 17
Is Jackson Martinez an outstanding talent? Yes. Of course. But
he lacked maybe little bit quality after "Thriller".

Wenger Knows Best @wengerknowsbest · Jan 18
Arsenal 2 Fulham 0 I believe today our occasional tactic to
drop little bit physically in the first half maybe lulled Fulham
into a false sense of security.

Wenger Knows Best @wengerknowsbest · Jan 19
I have been little bit quiet since the match, as I've been up all
night being active in the market. Vucinic? Not especially.

Wenger Knows Best @wengerknowsbest · Jan 19
Who do I want to win between Chelsea and Utd? I don't know.
I hope they both lose. Have I said that before? Yes. Is it still
funny? Yes.

January 2014

Wenger Knows Best @wengerknowsbest — Jan 19
I believe it is still too early to talk of United winning the Championship. They might still avoid relegation to it.

Wenger Knows Best @wengerknowsbest — Jan 19
Do United need to rebuild their team completely? No. Not necessarily. I believe they need only maybe 10-11 players.

Wenger Knows Best @wengerknowsbest — Jan 20
I don't like Le Ballon d'Or. I don't like Le Piat d'Or. I don't like Hors D'Oeuvres. Overall, I don't like d'Ors.

Wenger Knows Best @wengerknowsbest — Jan 20
I must say, I did quite like Diana d'Ors. And the film Sliding D'Ors. And the American band The d'Ors. Jim Morrison had exceptional quality.

Wenger Knows Best @wengerknowsbest — Jan 21
We are currently still up, day and night, being super active in the market. Are we close to signing anybody? Not especially.

Wenger Knows Best @wengerknowsbest — Jan 21
Might we create little bit smokescreen to deflect attention from real targets? I don't know. But I must say, Berbatov has super quality.

Wenger Knows Best @wengerknowsbest — Jan 21
Is Rosicky going to Bayern Munich? I must tell you, yes. It is true. Tuesday 11th March, 7.45. We are all going.

Wenger Knows Best @wengerknowsbest — Jan 21
Is Bendtner's choice this summer still between Barcelona and Madrid? Yes. I must say that is true. But he can go where he likes on holiday.

January 2014

Wenger Knows Best @wengerknowsbest — Jan 21
Am I close to a new contract? Yes. For example, I signed the last one only a few years ago.

Wenger Knows Best @wengerknowsbest — Jan 21
If I sign a new contract with this club might I move upstairs after? Yes. If there is a penthouse flat, I will do it.

Wenger Knows Best @wengerknowsbest — Jan 22
I believe criticism of West Ham losing 9-0 on aggregate to Man City is little bit harsh. Even Barcelona lost 7-0 to Bayern Munich.

Wenger Knows Best @wengerknowsbest — Jan 22
Might West Ham sack Allardyce? I believe it is too early for that. We don't play them until April 12th and we will be up for it.

Wenger Knows Best @wengerknowsbest — Jan 23
Well, sending that lookalike to Heathrow yesterday looks to have thrown everybody off little bit scent.

Wenger Knows Best @wengerknowsbest — Jan 23
Is my lookalike, Barry, available for weddings and barmitzvahs? I don't know. I must say, he enjoyed that waterslide a few years ago.

Wenger Knows Best @wengerknowsbest — Jan 23
I must tell you, we do not laugh at Manchester United. Absolutely no. At least not publicly.

Wenger Knows Best @wengerknowsbest — Jan 23
Bendtner in, Rosicky out. In out in out, shake it all about. I know more about Coventry, than you think. That's what it's all about.

January 2014

Wenger Knows Best @wengerknowsbest — Jan 23
I know much more than you think about Coventry. For example, its roots go back to little bit Saxon nunnery in AD 700.

Wenger Knows Best @wengerknowsbest — Jan 23
I feel little bit guilty I have no lunch news. I am running out of time to have lunch but if I can find something exceptional I will eat it.

Wenger Knows Best @wengerknowsbest — Jan 23
I can confirm that I have now eaten an undisclosed lunch, of undisclosed quality. Was it exceptional? I cannot disclose that.

Wenger Knows Best @wengerknowsbest — Jan 23
We are not close to signing anybody. If something exceptional turns up, of course we will do it. Excuse me, that is the door.

Wenger Knows Best @wengerknowsbest — Jan 23
"Arsène! Someone is here to see you..." "...Is it someone exceptional, darling?......Good evening Julian! How nice of you to turn up!..."

Wenger Knows Best @wengerknowsbest — Jan 24
We must be super careful not to disclose transfer targets, in case Chelsea try to sign them. I must say, Marlon Harewood has top quality.

Wenger Knows Best @wengerknowsbest — Jan 24
We look forward now to an undisclosed match against an undisclosed opponent at an undisclosed location. Tonight? I cannot disclose that.

Wenger Knows Best @wengerknowsbest — Jan 24
"Morning Ivan. Yes, I believe everyone bought that I was at Heathrow. Let's send Barry to little bit random game in Europe this weekend!"

January 2014

Wenger Knows Best @wengerknowsbest — Jan 24
"If Barry can consistently set a consistent smokescreen for the smokescreen Ivan, then we can concentrate on signing *undisclosed."

Wenger Knows Best @wengerknowsbest — Jan 24
Is Mourinho fair to contest my comments with a fresh argument? I don't know. I don't want to comment on floccinaucinihilipilification.

Wenger Knows Best @wengerknowsbest — Jan 24
Arsenal 4 Coventry City 0 The final score tonight was Arsenal undisclosed Coventry City undisclosed. Thank you for your interest in our affairs.

Wenger Knows Best @wengerknowsbest — Jan 24
Did we suffer tonight maybe little bit floodlight niggle? I don't know. I don't want to comment on illumination.

Wenger Knows Best @wengerknowsbest — Jan 25
Is today Saturday? I don't know. There are seven days in the week. We don't rule it out, but at the moment I can't announce anything.

Wenger Knows Best @wengerknowsbest — Jan 25
Jenkinson has no handbrake. Is he still running up and down the wing, making crosses, despite everyone having gone home last night? Yes.

Wenger Knows Best @wengerknowsbest — Jan 25
I believe Podolski is a natural clinical finisher. As soon as he sees a photographer, he smiles immediately with his thumbs up.

Wenger Knows Best @wengerknowsbest — Jan 25
Might there be little bit statue of Podolski outside the stadium in the future, smiling with his thumbs up? Why not?

January 2014

Wenger Knows Best @wengerknowsbest — Jan 25
Are we in for Mirko Vucinic? No. We would like a striker, yes, but I merely told Gazidis there "might not be much in it".

Wenger Knows Best @wengerknowsbest — Jan 26
Is Julian Draxler the new Thierry Henry? I must say, no. He is the current Julian Draxler.

Wenger Knows Best @wengerknowsbest — Jan 26
Is the rain exceptionally consistent? I don't want to comment on precipitation. But I believe Noah just went past on his Ark.

Wenger Knows Best @wengerknowsbest — Jan 26
Is it true there has been little bit transfer niggle and, due to a small confusion, Gazidis is trying to sign Juan Direction? No.

Wenger Knows Best @wengerknowsbest — Jan 27
Is Sagna going to Man City? I don't know, but probably yes. Second weekend in March, FA Cup 6th round, if we beat Liverpool.

Wenger Knows Best @wengerknowsbest — Jan 27
We can confirm that an undisclosed player has left this club to join an undisclosed club for an undisclosed fee.

Wenger Knows Best @wengerknowsbest — Jan 27
Does this undisclosed fee allow us now to offer more for an undisclosed player at another undisclosed club? I cannot disclose that.

Wenger Knows Best @wengerknowsbest — Jan 27
I don't know Puma.

January 2014

Wenger Knows Best @wengerknowsbest — Jan 27
We are delighted to disclose an undisclosed deal for an undisclosed kit. Thank you for your interest in our affairs.

Wenger Knows Best @wengerknowsbest — Jan 27
Will this new Puma deal include a new coat, to solve my little bit zip niggle? I don't know.

Wenger Knows Best @wengerknowsbest — Jan 28
We play tonight an undisclosed match at an undisclosed venue against undisclosed opponents. Are we up for it? I cannot disclose that.

Wenger Knows Best @wengerknowsbest — Jan 28
If my new contract is announced on Friday evening, after no transfers, would it be like a new signing? I don't know.

Wenger Knows Best @wengerknowsbest — Jan 28
Southampton 2 Arsenal 2 The final score tonight was Undisclosed undisclosed Undisclosed undisclosed. Thank you for your continued support.

Wenger Knows Best @wengerknowsbest — Jan 28
I believe, on reflection, that maybe our surprise tactic of dropping little bit physically in the first half did not really work.

Wenger Knows Best @wengerknowsbest — Jan 28
We are disappointed not to win tonight, yes of course, but mathematically I believe we still have a small chance to win the championship.

Wenger Knows Best @wengerknowsbest — Jan 28
I feel Flamini's red card was little bit harsh. Yes it was two-footed, because he was running, but he was not running violently.

January 2014

Wenger Knows Best @wengerknowsbest   Jan 29
Do we have a delegation in Germany negotiating a transfer?
I don't know. I thought Gazidis only popped out to get little
bit milk.

Wenger Knows Best @wengerknowsbest   Jan 29
"Hello?...Gazidis? It is little bit bad line. Where are you?...
Where?......Transylvania? No no no....I said Draxler. Draxler!..."

Wenger Knows Best @wengerknowsbest   Jan 29
Have I made a decision on what I shall eat for dinner?
No. I don't rule it out, but at the moment I cannot
announce anything.

Wenger Knows Best @wengerknowsbest   Jan 29
Well I must say, I forgot we had friends over tonight for
Draxler. I mean, dinner. Was it an exceptional evening? I'm not
telling you.

Wenger Knows Best @wengerknowsbest   Jan 30
Am I active on the lunch market? Yes. Am I close to eating
any? No. We are a long way apart.

Wenger Knows Best @wengerknowsbest   Jan 30
We are currently super exceptionally active in the market. I can
assure you, we will be working day and night, night and day
all night.

Wenger Knows Best @wengerknowsbest   Jan 30
Is there little bit Draxler niggle? Yes. Schalke want £37m, I
want to pay £37. Negotiations continue.

Wenger Knows Best @wengerknowsbest   Jan 31
Are we in for Kim Kallstrom? I don't know. Although I must say,
she showed outstanding quality in Baywatch.

Wenger Knows Best @wengerknowsbest — Jan 31

Aaron Ramsey has joined Elite London Model Agency for an undisclosed fee. We thank him for his contribution to this club.

Wenger Knows Best @wengerknowsbest — Jan 31

Has Frimpong joined Barnsley? Yes. We wish him well. Will he find Barnsley dench? We wish him well.

Wenger Knows Best @wengerknowsbest — Jan 31

Are we still in for a striker? Yes. If we can find one, we will do it. Have we joined the race for Danny Graham? There is a race?

Wenger Knows Best @wengerknowsbest — Jan 31

Is Dick Law in Italy for little bit striker deal? I don't know. I thought Dick Law was a detective show on Channel 5.

Wenger Knows Best @wengerknowsbest — Jan 31

You say Mor-ayta I say Mor-ata, let's call the whole thing little bit back on again? I don't want to comment on speculation.

Wenger Knows Best @wengerknowsbest — Jan 31

We are now very close to a new striker. Mitroglou has signed for Fulham and they are only about eight miles away.

Wenger Knows Best @wengerknowsbest — Jan 31

We are delighted to announce that an undisclosed player has joined on an undisclosed contract. What do you mean you know already?

Wenger Knows Best @wengerknowsbest — Jan 31

Kallstrom has outstanding technique, fantastic passing & exceptional hair. Footballistically, he offers consistently consistent versatility.

January 2014

Wenger Knows Best @wengerknowsbest · Jan 31
Kallstrom can do little bit holding role, play in the hole, 2nd striker, up front and used to like rush goalie at school.

Wenger Knows Best @wengerknowsbest · Jan 31
Did we have loan bids turned down for Kalou and Klose? No. Did we try to get Cisse from Newcastle? No. Is today Friday? No.

Wenger Knows Best @wengerknowsbest · Jan 31
We are little bit short on strikers, yes, I accept, but I didn't want to kill Bergkamp's statue, before we have even put it up.

Wenger Knows Best @wengerknowsbest · Jan 31
We should be alright for strikers. There is Giroud, Bendtner, Ozil, Sanogo, Merson, Nicholas and Draxler. I mean Drake.

I can now reveal the full story behind Frimpong's exciting move to Barnsley. Is the move dench? I don't know dench.

Frimpong came to see me and I told him I had accepted an offer. He joked he only wanted to go to Nando's or KFC, but I admitted that Kilmarnock had not come in for him.

"Is it Barcelona boss?"

"Well errr, no. But it has a similar spelling."

"Basel!?!"

"Barnsley."

"BARNSLEY!?!"

"They have exceptional potential. Congratulations."

Why do I always seem to suffer little bit zip niggle?

I don't know.

I must say, I don't understand why it fascinates
everybody. Overall, I feel the criticism is little
bit harsh.

Is it true that my big coat is officially the tallest coat
ever recorded, at 3.4 miles high?

I don't know about that. It must be little bit
optical illusion.

Why don't I just do my coat up before I go out onto
the pitch?

......That's not a bad idea.

"Arsène? Brendan Rodgers. I'm on the hands-free. Okay?…"

"……Good evening Brendan. And how are you?…"

"I'm absolutely terrific to be truthful with you Arsène. I'm looking forward to you visiting our fortress on Saturday!…It's a special fortress."

"Well yes, me too. I must tell you, we will be up for it!…Don't worry about Suarez, we won't try to sign him!"

"As I say, we're not worried Arsène. We've no special security plans in place.…We'll just maybes lower him onto the pitch from a helicopter…and have a wee armed guard with him at all times. Okay."

"Well err, I don't know about that. Overall, I must say I am little bit confused. You said 'As I say', but you had not already said the thing that you then said."

"…Okay. Terrific."

February 2014

Wenger Knows Best
@wengerknowsbest

Flamini in, Cazorla out. In out in out, shake it all about. You try not to lose 5-1 and you turn around, that's what it's all about.

14/02/2014

February 2014

Wenger Knows Best @wengerknowsbest   Feb 1
Well I must say personally I am delighted that the window is now closed. It was starting to get little bit chilly.

Wenger Knows Best @wengerknowsbest   Feb 1
Is the news true about Kallstrom? It is little bit un-com-fort-able to say, but I must tell you, yes. Sadly, he is not a striker.

Wenger Knows Best @wengerknowsbest   Feb 1
Is Kallstrom out for 2-3 months? I don't know. I believe he has just little bit "what-do-you-mean-he-already-had-a-back-niggle?" niggle.

Wenger Knows Best @wengerknowsbest   Feb 2
We are up for it. Crystal Pulis have improved, we know that. We are sure to cross some problems but we Tony concentrate on our own game.

Wenger Knows Best @wengerknowsbest   Feb 2
Is van Persie coming back to this club? I don't want to comment on individual players. But yes. February 12th, 7.45. If fit for Utd.

Wenger Knows Best @wengerknowsbest   Feb 2
The fans will cut slack for Chamakh coming back, he'll attack with a knack but will lack the fans' flack unless there's a fight back.

Wenger Knows Best @wengerknowsbest   Feb 2
Arsenal 2 Crystal Palace 0 A pinch and a Puncheon, 2nd day of the month. No returns. 2-0.

Wenger Knows Best @wengerknowsbest   Feb 2
I feel criticism of Kolo Toure is little bit harsh. As through-balls go, his pass directly to the feet of Anichebe was exceptional.

February 2014

Wenger Knows Best @wengerknowsbest · Feb 3
As we say in Alsace-Lorraine "If you make your bed little bit,
don't go complaining later if David Moyes lies in it."

Wenger Knows Best @wengerknowsbest · Feb 3
I remain absolutely convinced Kallstrom will be ready by late
February, in the middle of March, next April.

Wenger Knows Best @wengerknowsbest · Feb 3
I feel criticism of signing Kallstrom is little bit harsh. He has
only a small micro-fracture & we have all had them. Now
watch this drive.

Wenger Knows Best @wengerknowsbest · Feb 3
Pellegrini will be little bit low tonight. He did not see that
coming. He thought Branislav Ivanovic was a ladies
tennis player.

Wenger Knows Best @wengerknowsbest · Feb 5
I must say, I am little bit surprised Swansea have sacked
Laudrup. He has exceptional quality, fantastic spirit and
outstanding hair.

Wenger Knows Best @wengerknowsbest · Feb 5
I feel it is a small shame that Meulensteen is under little bit
pressure. Especially as we have played Fulham twice already.

Wenger Knows Best @wengerknowsbest · Feb 5
Was there little bit Pietersen dressing-room niggle? I don't
want to talk about individual players. Is he available on a free
loan? No.

Wenger Knows Best @wengerknowsbest · Feb 5
Will Ashley Cole re-join in the summer? No. I must say, when I
heard that little bit speculation I nearly swerved off the road.

February 2014

Wenger Knows Best @wengerknowsbest   Feb 6
Do I respect Liverpool? Of course. I have all The Beatles' albums. And I must say, Brookside was exceptional. Little bit Jimmy Corkhill.

Wenger Knows Best @wengerknowsbest   Feb 6
Do referees favour Liverpool? I don't know about that. I prefer to believe they do not get by with little bit help from our friends.

Wenger Knows Best @wengerknowsbest   Feb 6
Will we go for Suarez this summer? At the moment, no. Is it summer at the moment? No. Might we go for him when it is? I don't know summer

Wenger Knows Best @wengerknowsbest   Feb 6
Did Mark Austin suffer maybe little bit ITV autocue niggle tonight? I don't know. I don't want to comment on individual newsreaders.

Wenger Knows Best @wengerknowsbest   Feb 7
Do I do my food shopping at Tesco? I don't want to comment on supermarket speculation. But every little bit helps.

Wenger Knows Best @wengerknowsbest   Feb 7
Our new striker Yaya Sanogo played one hour today for our under-21s, after little bit long-term back niggle. How new is new? New enough.

Wenger Knows Best @wengerknowsbest   Feb 7
Will Suarez be a distraction tomorrow? No. We are up for it. We will have little bit dinner, relax and keep our minds focused.

Wenger Knows Best @wengerknowsbest   Feb 7
"Would I like wine with our meal? Errr yes why not? I'll have little bit nice bottle of Suarez. I mean, Shiraz. Thank you..."

February 2014

Wenger Knows Best @wengerknowsbest · Feb 7
"...Mr Wenger, Sir. More Shiraz?" "...More Suarez?" "Shiraz."
"Suarez." "Shiraz, Sir...More wine?" "...At the moment, no."

Wenger Knows Best @wengerknowsbest · Feb 7
Is Ribery a small doubt for our matches with Bayern? I believe
yes. But I don't like to talk about individual buttock niggles.

Wenger Knows Best @wengerknowsbest · Feb 8
We look forward to seeing Kolo Touré today. Is he currently
suffering maybe little bit form niggle? We look forward to
seeing him.

Wenger Knows Best @wengerknowsbest · Feb 8
Liverpool 5 Arsenal 1 The final score from Anfield was
Liverpool undisclosed Arsenal undisclosed. Did we lose 5-1?
No.

Wenger Knows Best @wengerknowsbest · Feb 8
Our fan belt today was exceptional. Un-com-fort-ably we
suffered little bit quadruple handbrake-gearbox-petrol-
sharpness niggle.

Wenger Knows Best @wengerknowsbest · Feb 8
We are exceptionally low tonight. We did not see that coming.
We were absolutely convinced Dean Sturridge had retired.

Wenger Knows Best @wengerknowsbest · Feb 8
Did I slip over at Lime Street Station before catching our train
home? No. I don't know streets, I don't know stations, I don't
know limes.

Wenger Knows Best @wengerknowsbest · Feb 9
I feel at Anfield on reflection we were little bit offensively
offensive and defensively offensive. Basically, we
were offensive.

February 2014

Wenger Knows Best @wengerknowsbest — Feb 9
Well errr I have had better weekends! But if you don't laugh you cry. Maybe I should check my Lottery ticket, to see if 5-1?

Wenger Knows Best @wengerknowsbest — Feb 9
Overall I feel the idea to slip over at Lime Street, to deflect little bit attention from our defeat, looks to have worked quite well.

Wenger Knows Best @wengerknowsbest — Feb 10
"Gazidis? Morning. Why is a juggler at our training ground?... What?...No no no...I said against Utd, we must go for the JUGULAR..."

Wenger Knows Best @wengerknowsbest — Feb 10
Franck Ribery still has little bit buttock niggle. Did Yaya Touré kick him? I don't want to comment on unanimous decisions.

Wenger Knows Best @wengerknowsbest — Feb 11
We are close now to a new contract for Sagna. Manchester City are quite interested and they are only 200 miles away.

Wenger Knows Best @wengerknowsbest — Feb 11
Do I believe criticism of Moyes is little bit harsh? I don't know. I let you know Thursday.

Wenger Knows Best @wengerknowsbest — Feb 11
Are there any changes for Utd? I don't know. But I must say, the fan belt did well at Liverpool and is in little bit contention to start.

Wenger Knows Best @wengerknowsbest — Feb 11
Can we afford any more slip-ups if we want to win the championship? I don't want to comment on Lime Street station.

February 2014

 **Wenger Knows Best** @wengerknowsbest · Feb 11
We want to treat the Liverpool game as an accident. Little bit like when we signed Squillaci? Similar.

 **Wenger Knows Best** @wengerknowsbest · Feb 11
I believe Moyes needs time and patience. I'm convinced of that. At least until Wednesday night anyway.

 **Wenger Knows Best** @wengerknowsbest · Feb 12
We are ready, we are up for it. We respect Man Utd. That's why we want to beat them.

 **Wenger Knows Best** @wengerknowsbest · Feb 12
"Ivan? Afternoon. Can you call the mechanic and ask him to remove little bit handbrake please and check the oil? Yes. Just take it off."

 **Wenger Knows Best** @wengerknowsbest · Feb 12
Have I refused to talk about having van Persie back at this club? No. I refuse to talk about refusing to talk about refusing it.

 **Wenger Knows Best** @wengerknowsbest · Feb 12
Arsenal 0 Manchester United 0 My players gave absolutely everything tonight. I feel the handbrake's petrol lacked maybe little bit sharpness. And it was windy.

 **Wenger Knows Best** @wengerknowsbest · Feb 13
We are delighted to announce the signing of Arsène Wenger on an undisclosed contract. Congratulations.

 **Wenger Knows Best** @wengerknowsbest · Feb 13
Well I believe that practice announcement went well. Have I already signed a new contract? I cannot disclose that.

February 2014

Wenger Knows Best @wengerknowsbest   Feb 13
After my new Arsenal contract ends will I move upstairs at the Emirates? I don't know. I must say, I'm quite happy in Totteridge.

Wenger Knows Best @wengerknowsbest   Feb 13
Should I have brought on extra substitutes against Utd? I don't know. But it is not too late, Sanogo is still warming up.

Wenger Knows Best @wengerknowsbest   Feb 13
I believe criticism of Giroud's quality against Utd is little bit harsh. The wind caused a small hairline fracture of the left quiff.

Wenger Knows Best @wengerknowsbest   Feb 13
Is it fair to say my "dithering and indecision is legendary"? I don't know. Well, no, it is little bit harsh. I have not decided.

Wenger Knows Best @wengerknowsbest   Feb 14
I wish everybody a Happy Valentine's Day. Although, of course, it is just little bit faux socio-economic consumer hegemony.

Wenger Knows Best @wengerknowsbest   Feb 14
Roses are red. Violets are blue. Nobody has better hair, than Olivier Giroud.

Wenger Knows Best @wengerknowsbest   Feb 14
We love you Arsenal, we do. We love you Arsenal, we do. We love you Arsenal, we do, as long as you don't lose.

Wenger Knows Best @wengerknowsbest   Feb 14
I must tell you, Liverpool are the first team I'd want to play after last Saturday. Sadly, Hyde FC were little bit unavailable.

February 2014

 **Wenger Knows Best** @wengerknowsbest — Feb 14
I am delighted to announce an agreement has been reached with Bacary Sagna and he has signed. Three autographs. At the training ground.

 **Wenger Knows Best** @wengerknowsbest — Feb 14
Flamini in, Cazorla out. In out in out, shake it all about. You try not to lose 5-1 and you turn around, that's what it's all about.

 **Wenger Knows Best** @wengerknowsbest — Feb 14
Mourinho feels I am a specialist in failure? I don't know. I have not gouged anybody's eyes. If that makes me a failure, I can accept that.

 **Wenger Knows Best** @wengerknowsbest — Feb 15
I do not have any hard feelings against Mourinho. I do not have any ill feelings against Mourinho. I do not have any feelings.

 **Wenger Knows Best** @wengerknowsbest — Feb 15
After little bit careful consideration, I have decided to play the best possible team against Liverpool. Brazil, 1970.

 **Wenger Knows Best** @wengerknowsbest — Feb 16
My players have rested well. We are super up for it and in high spirits. We are currently enjoying little bit pre-match knees-up.

 **Wenger Knows Best** @wengerknowsbest — Feb 16
"Nothing can look better than Mikel Arteta in the... mor-or-or-ning. Nobody looks taller than Santi Cazorla in the...mor-or-or-ning..."

 **Wenger Knows Best** @wengerknowsbest — Feb 16
Arsenal 2 Liverpool 1 Should Liverpool have had a second penalty? Yes, I agree, Gerrard should have been sent off.

February 2014

Wenger Knows Best @wengerknowsbest · Feb 16
Is Suarez little bit dramatic? I don't know. But his exceptional jazz hands give him outstanding potential for West End chorus lines.

Wenger Knows Best @wengerknowsbest · Feb 17
Should there have been another penalty? I accept, yes. Skrtel missed the ball and took out Cazorla's ankle. You're right, penalty.

Wenger Knows Best @wengerknowsbest · Feb 17
Does Suarez overact little bit? I believe yes. Could he have a future in Hollywood? Why not? He was exceptional in Platoon.

Wenger Knows Best @wengerknowsbest · Feb 17
Should Liverpool have had a stonewall penalty, for the challenge on Suarez? I don't know. Penalties are walls? Made from stone?

Wenger Knows Best @wengerknowsbest · Feb 17
I must tell you, there is no war of words between me and Mourinho. He has a war, I have words.

Wenger Knows Best @wengerknowsbest · Feb 18
Rosicky in, Arteta out. In out in out, shake it all about. You try not to lose 3-1 and you turn around, that's what it's all about.

Wenger Knows Best @wengerknowsbest · Feb 19
I remain absolutely convinced tonight we must show efficiently efficient efficiency, ruthlessly ruthless ruthlessness and not lose 3-1.

Wenger Knows Best @wengerknowsbest · Feb 19
Will Bayern use a false 9 tonight? I don't know. Might I use a false starting 11? I'm not telling you.

February 2014

Wenger Knows Best @wengerknowsbest   Feb 19
Arsenal 0 Bayern Munich 2 We are very very low tonight. We did not see that coming. We thought Gerd Muller had retired.

Wenger Knows Best @wengerknowsbest   Feb 19
I feel criticism of Özil is little bit harsh. He is just suffering at the moment from little bit cow's-bottom-banjo niggle.

Wenger Knows Best @wengerknowsbest   Feb 19
Did Robben and Neuer exaggerate contact purposely to get our players booked and sent off? I thought Sanogo played well.

Wenger Knows Best @wengerknowsbest   Feb 20
Did Tottenham win tonight in the Europa League? I don't know. I did not see the incident.

Wenger Knows Best @wengerknowsbest   Feb 21
I don't want to comment on Tottenham's opponents, but I feel in the second leg they may lack maybe little bit Petrovsk.

Wenger Knows Best @wengerknowsbest   Feb 21
We are still little bit low, but I believe we will give absolutely everything against Sunderland. Just not a penalty. Or a red card.

Wenger Knows Best @wengerknowsbest   Feb 21
At the moment we have to let Özil recover from missing the penalty. Are we dropping him from penalties? We are letting him recover.

Wenger Knows Best @wengerknowsbest   Feb 21
Monreal in, Gibbo out. In out in out, shake it all about. Nobody tell Johnson and you turn around, that's what it's all about.

February 2014

Wenger Knows Best @wengerknowsbest · Feb 22
We welcome back today Dennis Bergkamp, to unveil little bit statue. Has he brought his boots? I don't know. But I can ask.

Wenger Knows Best @wengerknowsbest · Feb 22
Arsenal 4 Sunderland 1 Sunderland were little bit unlucky today. Apart from our total domination and exceptional goals, there was not a lot in it.

Wenger Knows Best @wengerknowsbest · Feb 22
I believe Bergkamp's creative qualities are so exceptional he got two assists today just by sitting in the Directors' Box.

Wenger Knows Best @wengerknowsbest · Feb 22
Did Chelsea only beat Everton late today through diving near the penalty area until they got free-kicks? I don't want to comment on speculation.

Wenger Knows Best @wengerknowsbest · Feb 24
I am absolutely adamant Rosicky has to stay at this club. I am convinced of that. Hair like that is irreplaceable.

Wenger Knows Best @wengerknowsbest · Feb 24
Bergkamp's statue is an exceptional tribute to a player of outstanding quality. Even if it does have little bit pole-up-the-bottom niggle.

Wenger Knows Best @wengerknowsbest · Feb 24
Can we extend a small olive branch to Piers Morgan, after little bit chat-show-axe niggle? I believe yes. Gunnersaurus needs mucking out.

Wenger Knows Best @wengerknowsbest · Feb 24
Is Piers Morgan a "cock of the walk" today, or a "feather duster"? Pardon? I don't know.

February 2014

Wenger Knows Best @wengerknowsbest   Feb 25
Are Brad Guzan and Jonjo Shelvey little bit lookalikes? I feel maybe yes, but I don't know either of them.

Wenger Knows Best @wengerknowsbest   Feb 25
Do I believe Dennis Bergkamp will return to this club? Yes. One day. Monday? One day.

Wenger Knows Best @wengerknowsbest   Feb 25
We wish Joel Campbell well for Olympiacos against United, as he continues his recovery from little bit work permit niggle.

Wenger Knows Best @wengerknowsbest   Feb 25
I believe United will be little bit confused tonight. They thought Joel Campbell was a defender Rooney dived over in 2004.

Wenger Knows Best @wengerknowsbest   Feb 26
Have United turned a corner? I believe yes. Is it a good corner? I don't want to comment on speculation.

Wenger Knows Best @wengerknowsbest   Feb 26
Am I embarrassed for Mourinho saying the media should be embarrassed for him embarrassing himself? That might be embarrassing.

Wenger Knows Best @wengerknowsbest   Feb 27
Will I shake Mark Hughes's hand before the game at Stoke on Saturday? Yes, of course. Will I shake it after? I let you know.

Wenger Knows Best @wengerknowsbest   Feb 27
We are preparing well for Stoke. Mertesacker is showing exceptional quality at the line-out and Flamini is little bit natural scrum-half.

February 2014

Wenger Knows Best @wengerknowsbest · Feb 27
I must tell you, Stoke is always exciting. Their fans welcome me with little bit Mexican Wave. At least I think it's a welcome. And a wave.

Wenger Knows Best @wengerknowsbest · Feb 27
I apologise unreservedly for giving my players a two-day rest. I don't know what I was doing, I have only been in this job 30 years.

Wenger Knows Best @wengerknowsbest · Feb 28
We wish Spurs well in the Europa League. Might it drain their energy due to little bit futile won't-win-it-anyway niggle? We wish them well.

Wenger Knows Best @wengerknowsbest · Feb 28
Have I refused to rule out re-signing van Persie? No. Have I refused to rule out visiting the moon? No. But I have no plans for that either.

"Arsène? David Moyes..."
"...Right......Good evening David..."
"Sorry to trouble you at this moment in time, Arsène. I just wondered how you found your early days, at such a massive outfit like Arsenal Football Club."
"Well errr, you know, it was little bit difficult at first, but once my exceptional quality, fantastic attitude and outstanding mental strength came through, we won the double."
"Right.........It's just that people are saying I'm out of my league at United... Do you think I should resign?..."
"No. I remain absolutely convinced you are doing a fantastic job. I hope you stay there many years."

Vuelo
XL
IB
IB
IB
UY
JK
SK
RI

"Arsène? Brendan Rodgers.......Okay?…"

"Again?………What a lovely surprise to hear from you so soon. We've seen little bit of each other lately!…"

"Yeah it's been terrific! As I say, I just wanted to thank you for two great matches of such intensity and mentality. I thought our group was magnificent at Anfield."

"Well errr, yes, I must say personally I preferred our FA Cup win! We showed exceptional mental strength."

"You've got a terrific wee project there Arsène, no question. But our offensive power is something special. We could win our first title since 1990 to be truthful with you."

"Well, I don't like to comment on speculation. Overall I feel it is little bit too early to talk about winning the championship. Who knows, you might suffer little bit late title niggle and we win the FA Cup. I don't know."

"Ha ha. You've a terrific wee sense of humour Arsène!"

"…………Sorry, you're breaking up……"

March 2014

Wenger Knows Best
@wengerknowsbest

Has Adam been banned for stamping on Giroud? Yes. Can we go back to Stoke and restart against 10 men from 67 minutes? No.

05/03/2014

March 2014

Wenger Knows Best @wengerknowsbest Mar 1
We are ready for Stoke, we are up for it. Today's substitutes are Fabianski, Jenkinson, Gnabry, Chabal, O'Driscoll, Robinson and Lomu.

Wenger Knows Best @wengerknowsbest Mar 1
Stoke City 1 Arsenal 0 We are very very low tonight. We did not see that coming. I thought Jonathan Walters was a singer in Pink Floyd.

Wenger Knows Best @wengerknowsbest Mar 1
Did the referee gift Stoke a penalty? I believe yes. If we had known it was their birthday, we would have brought a card.

Wenger Knows Best @wengerknowsbest Mar 1
Despite the manner of our defeat at Stoke, I feel nobody can question our mental strength. Well, you can, but I don't want you to.

Wenger Knows Best @wengerknowsbest Mar 2
I believe Sunderland still have a small small small small chance to win the Capital One Cup.

Wenger Knows Best @wengerknowsbest Mar 2
We congratulate Sunderland on winning Best Supporting Role in a League Cup Final.

Wenger Knows Best @wengerknowsbest Mar 3
I am little bit surprised Gareth Bale did not win Best Special Effects at the Oscars for 'Last Season', but his brother was outstanding in American Hustle.

Wenger Knows Best @wengerknowsbest Mar 3
Oxlade-Chamberlain did not start at Stoke due to little bit did-not-pick-him-to-start been-in-this-job-30-years niggle.

March 2014

Wenger Knows Best @wengerknowsbest   Mar 3
Did Suarez have a £40m release clause? Yes. I told you that. Did John W Henry ignore it? I don't know. I know only Thierry Henry.

Wenger Knows Best @wengerknowsbest   Mar 4
We are delighted Mertesacker and Rosicky have signed new contracts. Has Sagna signed a new contract? Sorry, can't hear you.

Wenger Knows Best @wengerknowsbest   Mar 4
Was Mertesacker an Arsenal fan as a boy? Yes. Did the little boy inside scream for him to sign his new Arsenal deal? I don't know.

Wenger Knows Best @wengerknowsbest   Mar 4
Did Charlie Adam stamp intentionally on Giroud's leg? I don't know. Did Giroud intentionally leg butt Adam's studs? No.

Wenger Knows Best @wengerknowsbest   Mar 4
I believe Liverpool's loss of £50m is little bit un-com-fort-able. Especially as we were so keen to help them with £40m of it.

Wenger Knows Best @wengerknowsbest   Mar 5
There is little bit good news on Kallstrom. Leading specialists say if you take two a day, all symptoms should go away.

Wenger Knows Best @wengerknowsbest   Mar 5
Has Adam been banned for stamping on Giroud? Yes. Can we go back to Stoke and restart against 10 men from 67 minutes? No.

Wenger Knows Best @wengerknowsbest   Mar 6
I remain absolutely convinced in the magic of the FA Cup. Losing at home to Blackburn? Leaving out Arshavin? The other magic.

March 2014

Wenger Knows Best @wengerknowsbest — Mar 6
Is Wilshere now on the plane to Brazil? What, while injured
playing for England and maybe out for the season?
I don't know.

Wenger Knows Best @wengerknowsbest — Mar 6
We wish England well for the World Cup. I believe all my
players are unavailable that week.

Wenger Knows Best @wengerknowsbest — Mar 7
I must tell you, I feel like I do not remember a season like this
for injuries. Even our injuries appear to have injuries.

Wenger Knows Best @wengerknowsbest — Mar 7
"Morning Ian." "Arsène." "We want little bit compensation for
Agger injuring Wilshere." "You're havin a laff!" "Suarez should
cover it."

Wenger Knows Best @wengerknowsbest — Mar 7
Might Birmingham be stripped of the Carling Cup due to little
bit Carson Yeung niggle? I don't know. But it would be little
bit silverware.

Wenger Knows Best @wengerknowsbest — Mar 7
I feel the fans' song for Mertesacker is exceptional. I don't
share his taste in music, but yes I also believe he is a big
funky German.

Wenger Knows Best @wengerknowsbest — Mar 7
Vermaelen fit Koscielny doubt, in out in out shake it all about.
Big funky German and you turn around, that's what it's
all about.

Wenger Knows Best @wengerknowsbest — Mar 7
I must say, our capacity to have one player injured as
soon as another becomes fit is showing disappointingly
consistent consistency.

March 2014

Wenger Knows Best @wengerknowsbest   Mar 7
If Barcelona choose to sell Alex Song, we wish him well.
Would we try to sign him back? We wish him well.

Wenger Knows Best @wengerknowsbest   Mar 8
Is Everton a priority? Yes, we are up for it. We want to do well,
we want to qualify. Everybody wants to win the FA Champions
League Cup.

Wenger Knows Best @wengerknowsbest   Mar 8
There is petrol in the tank, the handbrake has been oiled and
the fan belt will be well lubricated before kick-off.

Wenger Knows Best @wengerknowsbest   Mar 8
Arsenal 4 Everton 1 We are grateful today to Giroud and
Arteta, for their outstanding finishing, exceptional calmness
and immaculate hair.

Wenger Knows Best @wengerknowsbest   Mar 8
We were little bit concerned that the Toffees could be sticky
today, but thankfully we were not left as the puddings.

Wenger Knows Best @wengerknowsbest   Mar 8
We look forward now to an FA Cup semi final, at Wembley
Stadium. Will Arshavin play this time? Still no.

Wenger Knows Best @wengerknowsbest   Mar 9
Nothing could look better than Giroud and Arteta in
the...mor-or-or-ning.

Wenger Knows Best @wengerknowsbest   Mar 9
They are both more sparkly than the shooting of Ross Barkley
in the...mor-or-or-ning.

I must say, I respect international football very much,
but it is little bit like a dinner guest that does not
know quite when to leave.

A small chat, little bit food and fine wine of
exceptional quality and then you can't get rid of it.
It can become little bit un-com-fort-able.

"Well yes, it's been nice seeing you."

"Thanks for coming."

"Bye now. Bye."

"Bye."

"….Look, bye."

March 2014

 **Wenger Knows Best** @wengerknowsbest   Mar 9
Do Manchester City still have a small small chance to win the FA Cup? Frankly, no.

 **Wenger Knows Best** @wengerknowsbest   Mar 9
We respect Wigan but, I must tell you, we are not counting any FA Cup chickens. Largely because we do not have any chickens.

 **Wenger Knows Best** @wengerknowsbest   Mar 10
Bouldy used "Except" on Travel Scrabble during the flight to Munich. I added 7 letters for "Exceptionally" on little bit triple word tile. 142 points.

 **Wenger Knows Best** @wengerknowsbest   Mar 10
Vermaelen in, Gibbo out. In out in out, shake it all about. 11 v 11 and you turn around, that's what it's all about.

 **Wenger Knows Best** @wengerknowsbest   Mar 10
I must tell you, we have won everywhere in Europe. Apart maybe from the Nou Camp. And Napoli. And maybe little bit Stade de France.

 **Wenger Knows Best** @wengerknowsbest   Mar 11
I'm too tired now to play Bouldy on the Travel Cluedo. I hallucinated little bit and guessed Mourinho in the Boardroom with the Dossier.

 **Wenger Knows Best** @wengerknowsbest   Mar 11
My players are resting, some are having little bit kip. Tonight I remain convinced we will give absolutely everything, we are up for it.

 **Wenger Knows Best** @wengerknowsbest   Mar 11
Bayern Munich 1 Arsenal 1 I don't know Bayern Munich.

March 2014

Wenger Knows Best @wengerknowsbest • Mar 11
Bayern in Arsenal out, in out in out shake it all about. Take a touch, fall over and you turn around, that's what it's all about.

Wenger Knows Best @wengerknowsbest • Mar 11
If shoppers knock into Robben's trolley up the supermarket, does he roll on the floor looking plaintively to an assistant?
I believe yes.

Wenger Knows Best @wengerknowsbest • Mar 12
I don't want to criticise last night's referee. He started well, but maybe dropped little bit decisionally in the second half.

Wenger Knows Best @wengerknowsbest • Mar 12
We are still little bit low today. We did see that coming, but I've always preferred Batman anyway.

Wenger Knows Best @wengerknowsbest • Mar 12
We wanted to do well, we wanted to qualify, but I believe you don't always get what you deserve and you don't always deserve what you get.

Wenger Knows Best @wengerknowsbest • Mar 13
I am proud and delighted to announce that I have signed a new contract. Unlimited texts and 2Gb of data. Exceptional.

Wenger Knows Best @wengerknowsbest • Mar 13
Should I stay or should I go now? Should I stay or should I go now? If I go there will be trouble, if I stay we could win Double.

Wenger Knows Best @wengerknowsbest • Mar 13
Has Bendtner been involved in little bit taxi niggle in Denmark? I don't know. I did not see the incident.

March 2014

Wenger Knows Best @wengerknowsbest   Mar 14
Ramsey has had little bit small small setback. It is a setback
to the setback? Or a setback to the setback's setback?
I don't know.

Wenger Knows Best @wengerknowsbest   Mar 14
Mesut Özil Three To Four Weeks Away is three to four weeks
away from being four to six weeks away.

Wenger Knows Best @wengerknowsbest   Mar 14
Did Bendtner unbutton his trousers and abuse a taxi
driver? I don't know. I don't want to comment on individual
training methods.

Wenger Knows Best @wengerknowsbest   Mar 14
Rub a taxi in, rub a taxi out, in out in out shake it all about.
Whip it with a belt and you turn around, that's what it's
all about.

Wenger Knows Best @wengerknowsbest   Mar 15
Did Chelsea lose at Villa? Yes. Is this the beginning of
Mourinho specialising in failure? Maybe yes.

Wenger Knows Best @wengerknowsbest   Mar 15
Should the FA throw the book at Ramires, for his
unacceptable stamp on El Ahmadi? Yes. Perhaps the
heavy one.

Wenger Knows Best @wengerknowsbest   Mar 16
"Morning Sherwood. Yes, we're excited too. No, I don't
think anyone suspects anything. That coaching role? We let
you know."

Wenger Knows Best @wengerknowsbest   Mar 16
I remain absolutely convinced Kallstrom can have a major
impact this season. To his back, groin, or hamstring? Not that
sort of impact.

March 2014

Wenger Knows Best @wengerknowsbest — Mar 16
Tottenham 0 Arsenal 1 I feel overall today we were little bit jaded and lacked our normal fluidly fluid fluidity. But we showed resiliently resilient resilience.

Wenger Knows Best @wengerknowsbest — Mar 16
I believe Tottenham have little bit slogan niggle. To dare is to do? No. To dare is to dare. To do is to do. And we did it.

Wenger Knows Best @wengerknowsbest — Mar 16
"Evening, Sherwood. Yes, we enjoyed it too! That Chadli miss was little bit genius, thank you! Good luck as Norwich manager next season."

Wenger Knows Best @wengerknowsbest — Mar 17
To win at Tottenham was a massive three points for us. How massive? Massive. Massive enough? Look, they were massive.

Wenger Knows Best @wengerknowsbest — Mar 17
We wish a very happy birthday today to Pat Rice (65) and @ LeeDixon2 (50). Did I get them anything special? Yes. A 1-0 win at Tottenham.

Wenger Knows Best @wengerknowsbest — Mar 17
Has Moyes lost the United dressing room? I've heard nothing about that. Did he ever find it? I've heard nothing about that either.

Wenger Knows Best @wengerknowsbest — Mar 18
Have I made a decision about my future? Yes. Am I telling you? At the moment, no.

Wenger Knows Best @wengerknowsbest — Mar 18
We are delighted to announce Cazorla, Ramsey and Zelalem have signed new contracts. Was I tempted to join them? At the moment, no.

March 2014

Wenger Knows Best @wengerknowsbest — Mar 19
Do I have a £100m transfer kitty? I don't know. I don't even like cats.

Wenger Knows Best @wengerknowsbest — Mar 19
Well errr, I must say overall I believe I have shown exceptional commitment, fantastic leadership and outstanding hair.

Wenger Knows Best @wengerknowsbest — Mar 19
I feel criticism of Moyes so far is little bit harsh. I must say, we are quite happy with how he is doing.

Wenger Knows Best @wengerknowsbest — Mar 19
Utd did well tonight in the Champions League, we accept that. Was there a hat-trick of top quality? I did not see the incidents.

Wenger Knows Best @wengerknowsbest — Mar 20
We wish Utd well, after beating Olympiacos. Might it help them do us little bit favour against City next week? We wish them well.

Wenger Knows Best @wengerknowsbest — Mar 20
Have Utd reached another turning point? I don't know. I believe if you reach four turning points you are little bit back where you started.

Wenger Knows Best @wengerknowsbest — Mar 20
I must say, our fan belt is showing exceptional petrol and only little bit handbrake niggle in buying tickets for the FA Cup semi final.

Wenger Knows Best @wengerknowsbest — Mar 20
Can we beat Wigan to reach the FA Cup Final? I don't know. We want to do well, we want to qualify. We will give 5-1 absolutely everything.

March 2014

Wenger Knows Best @wengerknowsbest · Mar 20
Do I hope Chelsea mark my 1,000th game in charge with a special presentation? Yes. I hope they present me with all three points.

Wenger Knows Best @wengerknowsbest · Mar 21
How will I mark my 1,000th match with Arsenal? I don't know. I have been in this job 999 games, I don't have to justify every decision.

Wenger Knows Best @wengerknowsbest · Mar 21
Next 1,000 in, last 1,000 out. In out in out shake it all about. I'm not going that easily and you turn around, that's what it's all about.

Wenger Knows Best @wengerknowsbest · Mar 21
What is the secret behind my remarkable longevity at this club? That is hard to say. Probably not having left, or been sacked.

Wenger Knows Best @wengerknowsbest · Mar 22
I had little bit strange dream last night. It was my birthday and Mourinho asked me over to his house, but then he wouldn't let me in.

Wenger Knows Best @wengerknowsbest · Mar 22
I just had little bit small nuisance call. "Hello...?" "Arsène?" "... Jose?" "I sink you win today." "Wrong number."

Wenger Knows Best @wengerknowsbest · Mar 22
Chelsea 6 Arsenal 0 We stalled the engine after starting the ignition and the spark plugs failed, causing little bit catastrophic double triple breakdown niggle.

Wenger Knows Best @wengerknowsbest · Mar 22
I don't want to comment on the referee. But I believe he may have suffered little bit mistaken-identity-demoted-to-the-Championship niggle.

March 2014

 **Wenger Knows Best** @wengerknowsbest   Mar 22
We are extremely low tonight. We did not see that coming. We thought the Oscars were a few weeks ago.

 **Wenger Knows Best** @wengerknowsbest   Mar 22
Andre Marriner will be little bit low tonight. He did not see that coming. He meant to referee West Ham v Man Utd.

 **Wenger Knows Best** @wengerknowsbest   Mar 22
I have decided that overall the honourable thing to do is to resign. Myself. To watching Match Of The Day. Tonight. To see the incidents.

 **Wenger Knows Best** @wengerknowsbest   Mar 23
I had little bit strange dream last night. The players had lost a sick snail. How could we lose sick snail? I don't know.

 **Wenger Knows Best** @wengerknowsbest   Mar 23
Why is my Swansea press conference called off? I don't want to comment on speculation. But it takes time to announce a new contract.

 **Wenger Knows Best** @wengerknowsbest   Mar 23
Did I tell my players at the Chelsea game that I will leave at the end of the season? I must tell you, yes. Of course. There is a World Cup.

 **Wenger Knows Best** @wengerknowsbest   Mar 24
There is currently little bit rumour niggle. I did not tell the players I was resigning in May. I told them I was re-signing in May.

 **Wenger Knows Best** @wengerknowsbest   Mar 24
Bellerin, Bellerout, in out in out, shake it all about. Don't lose this one 6-0 and you turn around, that's what it's all about.

March 2014

Wenger Knows Best @wengerknowsbest   Mar 24
Did Chuba Akpom score a hat-trick today for our under-21s?
Yes. Is he like a new signing? Why not? Can he go back in
time and play at Chelsea? No.

Wenger Knows Best @wengerknowsbest   Mar 24
Akpom, Akpom, Chuba Akpom. Need to save our season
then a striker comes along. Akpom, Akpom, Chuba Akpom.
Chuba, you can join the squad.

Wenger Knows Best @wengerknowsbest   Mar 25
I must say, if you have little bit blocked nose I can recommend
Lockets. They have exceptional menthol strength.

Wenger Knows Best @wengerknowsbest   Mar 25
Was the Chelsea defeat an accident? Yes. I believe Chelsea
accidentally scored six goals.

Wenger Knows Best @wengerknowsbest   Mar 25
If I stay two more years I will be 20 years at Arsenal. I have
been in this job 18 years, I don't have to justify every decision.

Wenger Knows Best @wengerknowsbest   Mar 25
"Hello?" "Good morning Sir. Have you had some accidents
at work that weren't your fault?" "…Well errr, overall I
believe yes…"

Wenger Knows Best @wengerknowsbest   Mar 25
We welcome Swansea tonight. Will we give them a welcome
in the hillside? No. We don't have any hills. Maybe Tower Hill if
we don't win.

Wenger Knows Best @wengerknowsbest   Mar 25
My players have trained well for Swansea tonight, I can assure
you they are up for it. Was the training accidental? No.

March 2014

Wenger Knows Best @wengerknowsbest   Mar 25
Will our outfield players all wear the same home kit tonight?
Yes, of course. Might that confuse the referee? I don't know.

Wenger Knows Best @wengerknowsbest   Mar 25
Arsenal 2 Swansea City 2 I don't know what happened
tonight. We played with little bit handbrake but lacked fuel
injection before Swansea accidentally drew.

Wenger Knows Best @wengerknowsbest   Mar 25
Did we get a good recovery tonight, after Chelsea? Overall,
apart from not playing very well other than for one minute, yes.

Wenger Knows Best @wengerknowsbest   Mar 26
We will fight to the end. Is now the end? No. Is it the beginning
of the end, or the end of the beginning? I don't know.

Wenger Knows Best @wengerknowsbest   Mar 26
Is Paul Scholes right that we are a million miles away from title
challengers? No. Chelsea have a chance and they are only six
miles away.

Wenger Knows Best @wengerknowsbest   Mar 26
We are still little bit very low tonight. We did not see that
coming. Any more accidents and we will have an emergency.

Wenger Knows Best @wengerknowsbest   Mar 26
I believe Kim Kallstrom showed great potential against
Swansea. He's changed little bit since Sex And The City, but
what can you do.

Wenger Knows Best @wengerknowsbest   Mar 27
Liverpool are well ahead now yes, we accept that. Can they
show consistently consistent consistency to stay there? I
don't know.

March 2014

Wenger Knows Best @wengerknowsbest   Mar 27
Well yes, Ramsey is progressing well. Overall, he should be back in a few more weeks, by the end of the season, come August.

Wenger Knows Best @wengerknowsbest   Mar 27
We are offering Sagna less money and years than City, but we are confident he will stay. Just like Nasri, Fabregas and the other one.

Wenger Knows Best @wengerknowsbest   Mar 27
If I learn little bit Manchester accent, might Sagna stay? I don't know if I could be mithered, but it would be proper tops our kid.

Wenger Knows Best @wengerknowsbest   Mar 28
Am I staying at this club? I have given my word. Which word have I given? I am not telling you.

Wenger Knows Best @wengerknowsbest   Mar 28
Abou Diaby Two To Three Weeks Away is two to three days away from being two to three months away.

Wenger Knows Best @wengerknowsbest   Mar 28
We look forward to City now, we are up for it. We are six days unbeaten, we will give absolutely everything.

Wenger Knows Best @wengerknowsbest   Mar 28
Does Diaby return to full training on April 1st? Yes. Is that an April Fool's joke? I let you know April 2nd.

Wenger Knows Best @wengerknowsbest   Mar 28
I have only really been beaten once this season. By Bouldie, on the Travel Scrabble, in Dortmund. I was little bit jaded.

Wenger Knows Best @wengerknowsbest   Mar 29
Have I hired a plane to trail little bit 'Self-sustaining one - Wenger in' message just before kick-off? No. But it's not a bad idea.

March 2014

Wenger Knows Best @wengerknowsbest   Mar 29
Arsenal 1 Manchester City 1 Are we now out of the title race?
Look, we are not in the driving seat, but you look up the road
and you check in your mirrors.

Wenger Knows Best @wengerknowsbest   Mar 29
Mourinho will be little bit low tonight. He did not see that
coming. He thought Crystal Palace was a chandelier shop.

Wenger Knows Best @wengerknowsbest   Mar 30
"Ivan? Yes. I know. Little bit un-com-fort-able. 4-0, Suarez was
exceptional again. Should we try £40,000,002?"

Wenger Knows Best @wengerknowsbest   Mar 30
I must tell you, we did not expect any favours today from
Fulham and Tottenham. Largely because we knew we
wouldn't get them.

Wenger Knows Best @wengerknowsbest   Mar 30
Everton are close, we accept that. Are they now our biggest
game of the season? No. All games are the same size, I am
convinced of that.

Wenger Knows Best @wengerknowsbest   Mar 31
"Ivan, evening. Southampton have £27m transfer debt?
Yes. Should we bid £27,000,001 for Lallana, Lambert and
Rodriguez? Probably not."

Wenger Knows Best @wengerknowsbest   Mar 31
"Ivan? Yes I arrived fine in Basel. No, I don't think anybody
saw me at Heathrow. Yes, *undisclosed would be exceptional
for us."

Wenger Knows Best @wengerknowsbest   Apr 1
I believe there is still a small small chance we can win the
championship. Is this little bit April Fools' joke? No, I mean it.

April 2014

Wenger Knows Best @wengerknowsbest — Apr 1
Will Bayern win tonight at Old Trafford? Yes, that's right, I do expect United to have a player sent off.

Wenger Knows Best @wengerknowsbest — Apr 1
Why did the Bayern Munich chicken cross the road? To get to the other dive.

Wenger Knows Best @wengerknowsbest — Apr 1
I must say, I feel little bit peckish tonight watching Barcelona v Atletico Madrid. I might open a small Pique of Busquets.

Wenger Knows Best @wengerknowsbest — Apr 2
I did not see the incidents, but I believe Man Utd have won the Champions League and Liverpool have won the Premier League. Congratulations.

Wenger Knows Best @wengerknowsbest — Apr 2
Did we fail to sign a Lille striker in January? Will we try again this summer? I don't know, I don't have a Kalou.

Wenger Knows Best @wengerknowsbest — Apr 2
Chelsea were little bit unlucky tonight. Apart from giving away goals and lacking class, quality and sharpness, there wasn't much in it.

Wenger Knows Best @wengerknowsbest — Apr 3
I feel criticism of David Luiz's own goal in Paris is little bit harsh. It was an exceptional finish of top top quality.

Wenger Knows Best @wengerknowsbest — Apr 3
Chelsea have little bit striker shortage niggle. They have only Torres, Eto'o, Ba and Lukaku at Everton. If only they had money to sign more.

Wenger Knows Best @wengerknowsbest — Apr 3
We welcome back Ramsey. I can assure you, we will not rush him. But if he can play the rest of the season that would be exceptional.

I had little bit strange dream last night.
Overall, I believe I might have been James Bond.

I was looking for some silverware that had been missing in action since 2005, after a new operation came into force, led by a Russian and a man from Portugal.

People say to me "Why do you talk about Arsenal like it is a motor car?"

So I tell them. "When you put in top quality petrol you do not expect the spark plugs to lack little bit sharpness, or to play with the handbrake on, otherwise the fan belt complains and blames niggles on the servicing department."

Why do we suffer so many injury niggles in recent years? I don't know. It is easy to blame the servicing department, but sometimes you just have to accept that the parts are little bit worn and you might have to buy a new model.

But I must tell you, it is not easy. We are active in the market, day and night, night and day. If we can find one or two new models of exceptional quality we will do it.

April 2014

Wenger Knows Best
@wengerknowsbest

Can we win the FA Cup? Yes. I am convinced of that. The semi-final and final are not early kick-offs, so we should be alright.

09/04/2014

April 2014

Wenger Knows Best @wengerknowsbest   Apr 3
Diaby is back. Also ankle, 8 times. Knee 4. Calf 11.
Thigh 5. Illness 2. Hamstring 3. Shin 2. Groin, abdomen
and concussion.

Wenger Knows Best @wengerknowsbest   Apr 4
Gibbs has an ankle problem. Gnabry has a knee problem. Do
Everton have a Ramsey problem? Footballistically, I hope yes.

Wenger Knows Best @wengerknowsbest   Apr 4
I believe we have turned a corner. Highbury Corner? Piebury
Corner? Müller Fruit Corner? I don't know. A corner.

Wenger Knows Best @wengerknowsbest   Apr 5
We are up for it. The race remains little bit unpredictable,
but I believe there is still a small chance we can win the
Grand National.

Wenger Knows Best @wengerknowsbest   Apr 5
Who will win the Grand National? I don't know. If you
look at form and quality, there can be only one winner.
Bayern Munich.

Wenger Knows Best @wengerknowsbest   Apr 6
If Peter has five apples and Mary has only 20 pence, do we
still have a small small chance to win the championship?
I believe yes.

Wenger Knows Best @wengerknowsbest   Apr 6
Is today an audition for Roberto Martinez? I don't know. Can
he replace Brucie, on Strictly? Yes, why not?

Wenger Knows Best @wengerknowsbest   Apr 6
Everton 3 Arsenal 0 I don't know what happened today. To
lose again heavily is hard to take. I cannot put my finger on
mental strength why this is happening.

April 2014

Wenger Knows Best @wengerknowsbest — Apr 6
What you cannot question is our commitment. My players gave absolutely everything. Possession, chances, three goals, points and momentum.

Wenger Knows Best @wengerknowsbest — Apr 6
Do my players lack little bit mental strength? I remain absolutely convinced you cannot say that. Well you can, but I don't want you to.

Wenger Knows Best @wengerknowsbest — Apr 6
We had petrol at Everton but our spark plugs failed and we had a major fuel leak. What is vital now is that our fan belt does not split.

Wenger Knows Best @wengerknowsbest — Apr 8
I can tell you, I will not walk away from this club. For £7.5m a year, I might find a taxi of exceptional quality.

Wenger Knows Best @wengerknowsbest — Apr 8
I still feel little bit down today. 3-0 down? 5-1 down? 6-0 down? I don't know. Just down.

Wenger Knows Best @wengerknowsbest — Apr 8
Am I keeping my staff and players in the dark? No. But I don't like to comment on illumination.

Wenger Knows Best @wengerknowsbest — Apr 8
Have I ever visited the special annual lights festival in Blackpool? I don't want to comment on illuminations.

Wenger Knows Best @wengerknowsbest — Apr 8
Can PSG win the Champions League next season? Yes, why not? If I can find players of super quality I will do it. I mean, they.

April 2014

Wenger Knows Best @wengerknowsbest · Apr 8
I remain absolutely committed to this club. I have given my word. Would I take over at PSG? No. Unless I decide otherwise.

Wenger Knows Best @wengerknowsbest · Apr 9
Early team news for Saturday is good. Undisclosed is alright. Undisclosed, undisclosed and undisclosed are okay. We are up for the Cup.

Wenger Knows Best @wengerknowsbest · Apr 9
Millwall beat Wigan 1-0 and I have a 100% record against Millwall, having never faced them. We will give absolutely everything.

Wenger Knows Best @wengerknowsbest · Apr 9
Can we win the FA Cup? Yes. I am convinced of that. The semi-final and final are not early kick-offs, so we should be alright.

Wenger Knows Best @wengerknowsbest · Apr 9
Do we have a Plan B? No. I believe if you have a Plan B, it shows that you do not respect Plan A.

Wenger Knows Best @wengerknowsbest · Apr 10
Rosicky has little bit thigh. Gibbs has little bit ankle. Does Oxlade-Chamberlain have little bit groin? Well, I don't know about that.

Wenger Knows Best @wengerknowsbest · Apr 10
Were Man Utd brave to lose to Bayern Munich? I don't know. Were we brave to lose to Bayern Munich? Or Barcelona, twice? Brave, no.

Wenger Knows Best @wengerknowsbest · Apr 11
We want to do well. We want to qualify. We respect the FA Cup very much. That's why we have given it little bit space for nine years.

April 2014

Wenger Knows Best @wengerknowsbest · Apr 11
I must tell you, we are ready prepared and super exceptionally up for it against Wigan. Do I still have a magic hat? I hope so.

Wenger Knows Best @wengerknowsbest · Apr 11
Tonight's Travel Scrabble game with Bouldie ended with a small small accident. He was about to win when I knocked it on the floor.

Wenger Knows Best @wengerknowsbest · Apr 12
I feel everybody is today maybe little bit nervous, but I can assure you my players are ready. We are super exceptionally up for it.

Wenger Knows Best @wengerknowsbest · Apr 12
We are well oiled, the engine has been serviced and we expect a fantastically strong fan belt today. Overall, I believe we will do it.

Wenger Knows Best @wengerknowsbest · Apr 12
If we lose to Wigan, might today be my swan song? I don't know. Do swans sing? No.

Wenger Knows Best @wengerknowsbest · Apr 12
Wigan 1 Arsenal 1 I must tell you, sometimes you must be super patient. We knew that Wigan drop little bit physically in the first half of penalties.

Wenger Knows Best @wengerknowsbest · Apr 12
Wigan played well, we know that, but we showed outstanding mental strength to fight to the end. Mertesacker was exceptionally exceptional.

Wenger Knows Best @wengerknowsbest · Apr 12
The fan belt gave absolutely everything and are right about Mertesacker. Big funky German! We've got a big funky German! Big funky Gerrrman!

April 2014

Wenger Knows Best @wengerknowsbest   Apr 13
I must tell you, beating Wigan has no bearing on my future.
Although, overall, I believe losing to them wouldn't have done
it any good.

Wenger Knows Best @wengerknowsbest   Apr 13
We congratulate Hull City on reaching the FA Cup Final. We
look forward to that. Might we change our name to Arsenal
London Cannons? No.

Wenger Knows Best @wengerknowsbest   Apr 13
Does Bubba Watson look little bit like Olivier Giroud?
Well yes, maybe little bit, but I don't like to comment on
individual golfers.

Wenger Knows Best @wengerknowsbest   Apr 14
Podolski is a small doubt for West Ham. Is he suffering from
little bit "don't-you-complain-about-being-substituted" niggle?
No.

Wenger Knows Best @wengerknowsbest   Apr 14
Criticism of Giroud is little bit harsh. He showed at Wembley
a fantastic spirit, exceptional physical strength and
outstanding hair.

Wenger Knows Best @wengerknowsbest   Apr 14
Are there enough FA Cup Final tickets for our fan belt?
Absolutely no. But I don't like to comment on ticket allocation.

Wenger Knows Best @wengerknowsbest   Apr 14
I believe we had 49,000 fans at the semi final and 25,000
tickets for the final. If we can put 24,000 fans on the bench we
will do it.

Wenger Knows Best @wengerknowsbest   Apr 15
We are already planning for next season, working day and
night, night and day on new signings. Are renewals out soon?
I don't know.

April 2014

Wenger Knows Best @wengerknowsbest · Apr 15

I can assure you, we are up for it tonight. Podolski is a small late doubt, with little bit double-thumbs-up-smile niggle.

Wenger Knows Best @wengerknowsbest · Apr 15

Might we surprise everybody tonight, with something little bit unexpected? I don't know. I don't want to comment Özil on speculation.

Wenger Knows Best @wengerknowsbest · Apr 15

Arsenal 3 West Ham 1 Well errr, I must say, I believe the plan to surprise West Ham by not taking off Podolski on 68 minutes worked little bit treat.

Wenger Knows Best @wengerknowsbest · Apr 15

We respect Jarvis for staying on his feet. We respect the referee for not giving a penalty. Overall, we respect West Ham for not winning.

Wenger Knows Best @wengerknowsbest · Apr 15

Are West Ham still forever blowing bubbles? At the moment, no.

Wenger Knows Best @wengerknowsbest · Apr 16

Have I told my players it is compulsory they win our remaining games? Yes. Should I have told them that in August? Yes.

Wenger Knows Best @wengerknowsbest · Apr 16

I must tell you, I believe Everton did not expect to lose to Crystal Palace tonight. Nobody expects the Pulis Inquisition.

Wenger Knows Best @wengerknowsbest · Apr 16

We congratulate Real Madrid on winning the Copa del Rey. Is it like a trophy? Well errr, it is no 4th place, but I believe yes.

April 2014

Wenger Knows Best @wengerknowsbest Apr 17
We will prepare super exceptionally for Hull. In this league, anybody can beat anybody. Can Hull beat us? Well, hopefully not anybody.

Wenger Knows Best @wengerknowsbest Apr 18
Hull City have the eye of the tiger, we accept that. But like in little bit paper-scissors-rock, a cannon beats a tiger.

Wenger Knows Best @wengerknowsbest Apr 18
Is my presence at last night's youth match a clue I am staying at this club? I don't know. I might have been there in my spare time.

Wenger Knows Best @wengerknowsbest Apr 18
I believe Aaron Ramsey deserves to win PFA Young Player of the Year, but we accept Daniel Sturridge has a dance of great potential.

Wenger Knows Best @wengerknowsbest Apr 19
We are ready for Sunday, we are up for it, but we accept it will be difficult. Are we prepared to go to Hull and back? Yes, of course.

Wenger Knows Best @wengerknowsbest Apr 19
I believe David Marshall of Cardiff City is a goalkeeper of outstanding quality. But I don't like to talk about individual players.

Wenger Knows Best @wengerknowsbest Apr 19
Mourinho will be desperately low tonight. He did not see that coming. He thought he'd loaned Fabio Borini to Vitesse Arnhem.

Wenger Knows Best @wengerknowsbest Apr 20
Is today little bit dress rehearsal for the FA Cup Final? Why not? Have we decided what dress we're wearing? Not that sort of rehearsal.

April 2014

Wenger Knows Best @wengerknowsbest   Apr 20
Hull City 0 Arsenal 3 I can tell you, Arteta is alright. He has suffered little bit lost-tooth niggle, but his hair is fine.

Wenger Knows Best @wengerknowsbest   Apr 20
Today we looked into the eye of the Tigers and we were survivors. Have I done that one before? Yes. But it is still little bit funny.

Wenger Knows Best @wengerknowsbest   Apr 20
I must tell you, Everton are showing no sign of going away. Which is little bit shame, as I do not remember inviting them.

Wenger Knows Best @wengerknowsbest   Apr 22
I believe Moyes was little bit unlucky at Utd. Apart from lacking maybe quality, tactics, results and points, he did quite well.

Wenger Knows Best @wengerknowsbest   Apr 22
Should Utd have given Moyes more time? I believe yes. Personally, I feel contracts should always be honoured.

Wenger Knows Best @wengerknowsbest   Apr 22
Could Moyes have stayed at Utd another five years? Yes. If only he had mentioned having little bit project, he might have been alright.

Wenger Knows Best @wengerknowsbest   Apr 22
Did Moyes lose the Utd dressing room? I don't know. Did he ever find the Utd dressing room? I don't want to comment on speculation.

Wenger Knows Best @wengerknowsbest   Apr 22
I must say, do not forget Moyes broke records at Utd that had stood for many years. Nobody else had achieved that.

April 2014

Wenger Knows Best @wengerknowsbest — Apr 22
Am I signing a new contract to stay at this club, or am I leaving in May? I don't know. I might have devised little bit project.

Wenger Knows Best @wengerknowsbest — Apr 22
Abou Diaby Two To Three Weeks Away is now fit and ready to play. Is he like a new signing? No. But he was eight years ago.

Wenger Knows Best @wengerknowsbest — Apr 22
I thought David Villa was going to head a late winning goal, but maybe he wanted to avoid little bit niggle with his exceptional hair.

Wenger Knows Best @wengerknowsbest — Apr 22
Might I go to Man Utd? I can tell you, no. We have played there already.

Wenger Knows Best @wengerknowsbest — Apr 23
I feel Atletico lacked maybe little bit fuel injection last night against Chelsea, but overall their fan belt was exceptional.

Wenger Knows Best @wengerknowsbest — Apr 23
Who do I want to win tonight, between Real Madrid and Bayern München? I don't know. I wouldn't want to dive in.

Wenger Knows Best @wengerknowsbest — Apr 23
Did Mourinho aim little bit striker dig at Abramovich to create confrontation for being freed to join Man Utd this summer? I don't know.

Wenger Knows Best @wengerknowsbest — Apr 23
Am I keeping tabs on Tom Cleverley? No. Could I use that as little bit smokescreen for keeping tabs on someone else? Yes.

April 2014

Wenger Knows Best @wengerknowsbest   Apr 24
Might Jenkinson go to Newcastle on loan next season? I don't know about that. Does he have Newcastle posters in his bedroom? No.

Wenger Knows Best @wengerknowsbest   Apr 24
Has Bacary Sagna heaped praise on Abou Diaby? Yes. Although he should be little bit careful, we don't want to cause any niggles.

Wenger Knows Best @wengerknowsbest   Apr 25
Diaby in, Diaby out, in out in out shake it all about. Little bit groin niggle and you turn around, that's what it's all about.

Wenger Knows Best @wengerknowsbest   Apr 25
I can tell you, Diaby's little bit groin niggle is only a very small small niggle. Will he be back by next season? I believe yes.

Wenger Knows Best @wengerknowsbest   Apr 25
Is the ball now in Sagna's court? Yes. Is he likely to hit it back? I don't know.

Wenger Knows Best @wengerknowsbest   Apr 25
Has Mertesacker developed little bit Cockney accent? I don't know. But his plates of meat are in right little bit two and eight.

Wenger Knows Best @wengerknowsbest   Apr 25
Do I have little bit sore throat niggle today? Well yes, but I am currently physically unable to comment on speculation.

Wenger Knows Best @wengerknowsbest   Apr 25
Am I staying at this club? Look, I have given my word. Which word did I give? I'm not telling you.

April 2014

Wenger Knows Best @wengerknowsbest Apr 25

Have I decided to stay at this club, yes or no? Look, yes. Yes. I am staying at this club. Unless I decide otherwise. And maybe back again.

Wenger Knows Best @wengerknowsbest Apr 26

I had little bit strange dream last night. I told everybody that I was staying at this club. I must say, it seemed so real.

Wenger Knows Best @wengerknowsbest Apr 26

Given my little bit croaky voice, Lockets have exceptional menthol strength. Do I have a competition lined up? No. But it's not a bad idea.

Wenger Knows Best @wengerknowsbest Apr 26

"Ivan? Yes I know, Everton. Little bit double own goal niggle! Should you put in a small small bid for Coleman? Yes, why not?"

Wenger Knows Best @wengerknowsbest Apr 27

We congratulate Luis Suarez on being named the PFA Player of the Year. He has played as well as Ramsey? No.

Wenger Knows Best @wengerknowsbest Apr 27

Liverpool were little bit unlucky today. Chelsea were offensively defensive and defensively offensive. Basically, they were offensive.

Wenger Knows Best @wengerknowsbest Apr 28

Will I shake Pardew's hand before tonight's game? Yes, of course. Will I wear protective headgear, boxing gloves and a mouth guard? No.

Wenger Knows Best @wengerknowsbest Apr 28

If it is too difficult for fans to get home tonight, due to little bit tube niggle, they could always stay for West Brom on Sunday.

April 2014

Wenger Knows Best @wengerknowsbest   Apr 28
Arsenal 3 Newcastle Utd 0 We are delighted to reach the Fourth Place Trophy Final. I can assure you, we will take West Brom very seriously. We are up for it.

Wenger Knows Best @wengerknowsbest   Apr 28
We had a good performance tonight, maybe little bit cautious. But once the engine warmed up, the fuel injection was outstanding.

Wenger Knows Best @wengerknowsbest   Apr 28
Ozil has suffered little bit physically in the second half of the season, but he looks sharp since returning from his handbrake niggle.

Wenger Knows Best @wengerknowsbest   Apr 28
I feel criticism of Newcastle is maybe little bit harsh. Apart from a total lack of quality, sharpness and defending they did alright.

Wenger Knows Best @wengerknowsbest   Apr 29
"Afternoon Sherwood....Yes, delighted to finish above Tottenham again, me too!...That coaching role next season? We let you know."

Wenger Knows Best @wengerknowsbest   Apr 29
Does Ancelotti have little bit eyebrow niggle? No. Is it a small imbalance in the fuel injection? I don't know, I'm not a mechanic.

Wenger Knows Best @wengerknowsbest   Apr 29
Bayern Munich will be very low tonight. They did not see that coming. They thought Sergio Ramos was still manager of Tottenham.

Wenger Knows Best @wengerknowsbest   Apr 30
Real Madrid showed exceptional quality to beat Bayern. Would Real have coped against Ramsey, Wilshere and Walcott? I believe no.

April 2014

Wenger Knows Best @wengerknowsbest — Apr 30
We congratulate Leicester and Burnley on being promoted.
We look forward to beating, sorry meeting, them next season.

Wenger Knows Best @wengerknowsbest — Apr 30
Chelsea and Atletico will want to do well, they both want to
qualify. I believe the best team will do it. But hopefully Atletico.

Wenger Knows Best @wengerknowsbest — Apr 30
I expect Chelsea to do well tonight, I expect them to qualify.
I didn't say I want them to, just that I expect it.

Wenger Knows Best @wengerknowsbest — Apr 30
Chelsea are out? If they now win nothing this season and I win
the FA Cup, am I still the specialist in failure? I don't know.

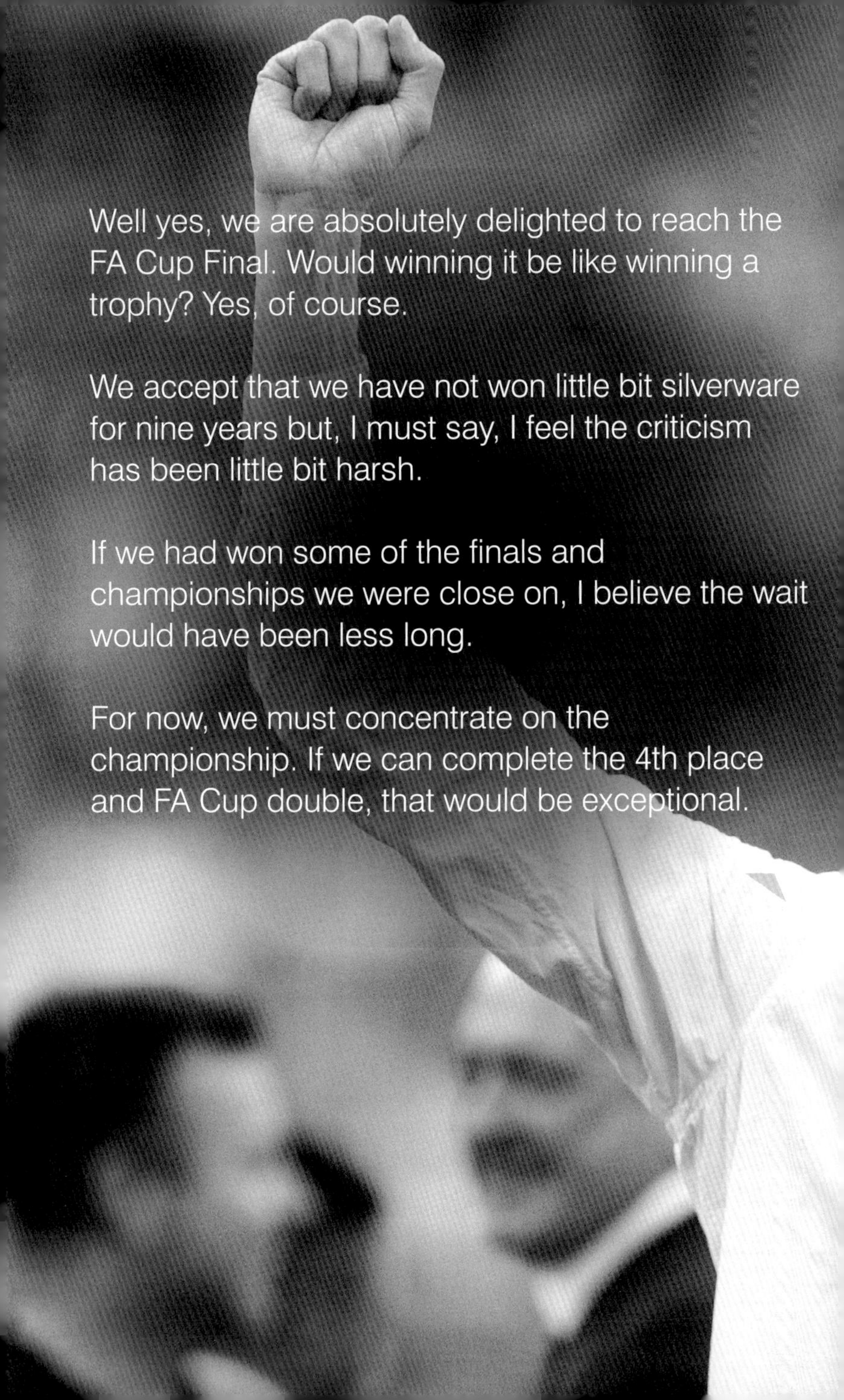

Well yes, we are absolutely delighted to reach the FA Cup Final. Would winning it be like winning a trophy? Yes, of course.

We accept that we have not won little bit silverware for nine years but, I must say, I feel the criticism has been little bit harsh.

If we had won some of the finals and championships we were close on, I believe the wait would have been less long.

For now, we must concentrate on the championship. If we can complete the 4th place and FA Cup double, that would be exceptional.

"Hello?.........Hello?...Is this a crossed line?…"

"…Arsène? Terrific!…It's Brendan!… And Jose is on the line too! It's a wee conference call, okay?…"

"….......Right….........You must be feeling little bit low Jose. I expect you did not see that Champions League exit coming?…"

"Yes. But I sink you know more about specialising in failure than me, Arsène!"

"Well errr, I don't know about that. Look, remind me, which cup final are you in? You might soon be two years without a trophy. Maybe you are the little bit apprentice in failure?"

"…Hey lads, lads! Okay. Listen, we're all part of a terrific wee football family here, okay! Maybes we'll see each other for the Community Shield?"

"Well, I must say, we hope to be there, yes. Although, overall, I think City might yet win the championship…"

May 2014

Wenger Knows Best
@wengerknowsbest

Arsenal 3 Hull City 2 I'm still little bit magic! I wear a magic hat! And when I saw the FA Cup, I said I'm having that!

17/05/2014

May 2014

Wenger Knows Best @wengerknowsbest　　May 1
A pinch and Jason Punchën, I might just have some lunchën, with little bit Bayern Munchën. No returns.

Wenger Knows Best @wengerknowsbest　　May 1
Am I having lunchën today with Jason Punchën and Bayern Munchën? Well, no, but it rhymed quite well. Little bit artistic licence.

Wenger Knows Best @wengerknowsbest　　May 1
When I said "Judge me in May", I did not necessarily mean this early in May.

Wenger Knows Best @wengerknowsbest　　May 1
Have Tottenham approached Frank De Boer? Or Frank de boer? Or Frank de Boer? I don't know. But correct capitals might be little bit vital.

Wenger Knows Best @wengerknowsbest　　May 2
Sagna is little bit doubt for the rest of the season. Frankly, I must tell you, Sagna is little bit doubt for the next three seasons.

Wenger Knows Best @wengerknowsbest　　May 2
I can tell you, Gibbs is very close and Wilshere is not far away. Overall, I think I might need new glasses.

Wenger Knows Best @wengerknowsbest　　May 2
Have I had lunch yet? No. I am not in for lunch at the moment. Would any particular food interest me? Not especially.

Wenger Knows Best @wengerknowsbest　　May 2
We are delighted to stage the Emirates Cup once again this summer. Will all our new signings be made in time? Yes of course.

May 2014

Wenger Knows Best @wengerknowsbest — May 2
Is Mourinho targeting two big summer signings? I don't know. But I believe Tomas Brolin and Neil Ruddock are available.

Wenger Knows Best @wengerknowsbest — May 3
Have I eaten breakfast yet? No. But I am active in the market and if I find one or two items of outstanding quality, I will do it.

Wenger Knows Best @wengerknowsbest — May 3
We are delighted to win the Fourth Place Trophy. To win it for 18 years takes consistently consistent consistency. Now for the Double.

Wenger Knows Best @wengerknowsbest — May 4
May the 4th be with us? Yes, of course. And tomorrow May the 5th will be with us. I don't know Star Wars.

Wenger Knows Best @wengerknowsbest — May 4
Arsenal 1 West Brom 0 We lacked today maybe little bit sharpness, but still showed enough pace from the gearbox to get a three-point endorsement.

Wenger Knows Best @wengerknowsbest — May 4
Was Loic Remy at our stadium today? Is he joining us for next season? I don't know. He might have just been here in his spare time.

Wenger Knows Best @wengerknowsbest — May 4
Overall, I don't know Loic Remy.

Wenger Knows Best @wengerknowsbest — May 5
Bacary Sagna has fantastic quality, an outstanding attitude and exceptional hair. Is he staying at this club? I don't know Serge Aurier.

May 2014

Wenger Knows Best @wengerknowsbest   May 6
Liverpool will be very very low today. They did not see that coming. They usually win on penalties when they draw 3-3.

Wenger Knows Best @wengerknowsbest   May 6
Would a UEFA fine and little bit squad limit stop Man City stockpiling players who no longer see the light of day? I don't know Jack Rodwell.

Wenger Knows Best @wengerknowsbest   May 6
Criticism of City stockpiling players to damage competition is little bit harsh. Nobody has forgotten Thingy Sinclair or Something Jovetic.

Wenger Knows Best @wengerknowsbest   May 7
Suarez crying was little bit un-com-fort-able. If he had joined this club, he would have an FA Cup Final to look forward to.

Wenger Knows Best @wengerknowsbest   May 7
Has Frimpong been released by Barnsley? Yes, we wish him well. Does he have a future back at this club? We wish him well.

Wenger Knows Best @wengerknowsbest   May 7
Does Podolski live at our stadium? Does his social media team take him there every day for little bit photoshoot? I don't know.

Wenger Knows Best @wengerknowsbest   May 7
Does Podolski have little bit doppelgänger, like I have Barry, smiling and holding up thumbs in different locations? Maybe yes.

Wenger Knows Best @wengerknowsbest   May 7
"Hello? Good evening Ivan. Should we have Barry call Frimpong and pretend to offer him a new deal? No no. That would not be dench."

May 2014

Wenger Knows Best @wengerknowsbest   May 8

I believe in a World Cup year, transfer business does not get done early. Especially if you leave it till late August.

Wenger Knows Best @wengerknowsbest   May 8

We have been top 128 days, which is basically half a season. Should we win half a championship and half a trophy? I believe yes.

Wenger Knows Best @wengerknowsbest   May 9

Can Helena Costa do well at Clermont Foot? Of course. Behind every successful manager is a successful womanager.

Wenger Knows Best @wengerknowsbest   May 9

It is little bit relief to have won Fourth Place already. We are grateful to Giroud, for hairing the winner against West Brom.

Wenger Knows Best @wengerknowsbest   May 9

Am I obsessed with hair? No. But I beweave if you perm our season's highlights and mullet over, they bob between quiffs and buts.

Wenger Knows Best @wengerknowsbest   May 9

Has Koscielny signed a new contract with this club? Yes. Can he sign Sagna's new contract too? I don't know about that.

Wenger Knows Best @wengerknowsbest   May 10

Monaco? No. There is little bit confusion over Monaco. I pulled over at Texaco. But only to put little bit petrol in the tank.

Wenger Knows Best @wengerknowsbest   May 10

Does the Eurovision Song Contest have top quality and outstanding potential? I don't know. I have successfully avoided the incident.

May 2014

Wenger Knows Best @wengerknowsbest — May 11
Can Norwich avoid little bit relegation niggle, by beating us 26-0? I don't know. We respect Norwich. That's why we want to beat them.

Wenger Knows Best @wengerknowsbest — May 11
Norwich City 0 Arsenal 2 We congratulate City on winning the championship. If it wasn't for inconsistently inconsistent inconsistency, it might have been us.

Wenger Knows Best @wengerknowsbest — May 11
I believe this season we have shown mostly consistently consistent consistency. Including away from home, against our rivals? Well, yes.

Wenger Knows Best @wengerknowsbest — May 11
We congratulate Spurs on 6th place. We wish them well in the Europa League. Might it keep them below us for a 20th year? We wish them well.

Wenger Knows Best @wengerknowsbest — May 11
We accept we have lacked petrol this season, but don't forget we did suffer little bit niggles to the handbrake, spark plugs and fan belt.

Wenger Knows Best @wengerknowsbest — May 11
I believe overall defensively we have shown outstanding brake pads, especially Mertesacker. Big funky German! We've got a big funky German!

Wenger Knows Best @wengerknowsbest — May 11
We are delighted for Jenkinson, on his first goal for this club. But, I must say, he has already scored hundreds in his dreams.

Wenger Knows Best @wengerknowsbest — May 12
Is it hard to sign players before the World Cup? Yes. How are Utd managing to sign Luke Shaw? I don't know. Have they signed him yet? No.

May 2014

Wenger Knows Best @wengerknowsbest   May 12
We wish Wilshere and Chamberlain well in England's squad for Brazil. Can they win the World Cup? We wish them well.

Wenger Knows Best @wengerknowsbest   May 12
I believe Jenko's omission from England's World Cup squad is little bit harsh. He is on an outstanding roll of one goal in one game.

Wenger Knows Best @wengerknowsbest   May 12
I believe Chelsea agreeing to pay £32m for Costa proves the market is inflated. Normally you can get a latte for £2.65.

Wenger Knows Best @wengerknowsbest   May 13
"Sherwood?...Oh right, good for you ...About 'that' coaching role? ...Sorry?...No, I didn't catch that... Little bit reception niggle..."

Wenger Knows Best @wengerknowsbest   May 14
We want to do well against Hull, we want to give absolutely everything. Apart from possession, goals and the FA Cup.

Wenger Knows Best @wengerknowsbest   May 14
Will we gift Hull a cup final winner, like we did Birmingham three years ago? I believe no. Have Hull signed Obafemi Martins? No.

Wenger Knows Best @wengerknowsbest   May 14
I must say, overall, we want to make our fans happy, we don't want them to be angry. You wouldn't like them when they're angry.

Wenger Knows Best @wengerknowsbest   May 14
We are delighted to announce that French international Cit Roën has signed a new long-term contract with this club.

May 2014

Wenger Knows Best @wengerknowsbest   May 14
Our new signing Cit Roën has top quality and a super engine.
Does it have little bit handbrake niggle? I don't know. I'm not
a mechanic.

Wenger Knows Best @wengerknowsbest   May 15
I believe talk of 9 years since our last trophy is little bit
disrespectful. It is only 4 years since we last won the
Emirates Cup.

Wenger Knows Best @wengerknowsbest   May 15
There is no room for complacency now, we know that. A
cannon should always beat a tiger, yes, but the cannon must
fire consistently.

Wenger Knows Best @wengerknowsbest   May 15
Complacency could risk a giant-killing to threaten all hopes
for little bit silverware. Wrexham? Well, it wouldn't do them
any good.

Wenger Knows Best @wengerknowsbest   May 15
Is it little bit presumptuous that we have a parade prepared
for Sunday? No. We have trained for the game on Saturday, is
that allowed?

Wenger Knows Best @wengerknowsbest   May 16
I hope everybody is little bit excited now it is FA Cup Final Eve.
The players are up for it. We'd quite like to play right now.

Wenger Knows Best @wengerknowsbest   May 16
We are making little bit final preparations. No high winds are
expected at Wembley, so Giroud's and Arteta's hair should be
fully fit.

Wenger Knows Best @wengerknowsbest   May 16
We have filled up on petrol, oiled the handbrake and
polished the gear stick. The fan belt should be well lubricated
by kick-off.

May 2014

 **Wenger Knows Best** @wengerknowsbest — May 16
Will Man City now limit transfer spending due to little bit FFP niggle? I believe yes. Will Sagna still join them? I don't know.

 **Wenger Knows Best** @wengerknowsbest — May 16
I wanted to smash Bouldie on the Travel Scrabble tonight but he wants to watch the MasterChef final. Little bit un-com-fort-able.

 **Wenger Knows Best** @wengerknowsbest — May 16
I must tell you, we are now super top super top super top top top super prepared for Hull. Is that arrogant? No. Just prepared.

 **Wenger Knows Best** @wengerknowsbest — May 17
Well that was little bit strange dream. A tiger was chasing me, but Poldi saved me, by smiling at it. What does it mean? I don't know.

 **Wenger Knows Best** @wengerknowsbest — May 17
Today we must all show exceptional mental strength. Engine, petrol, handbrake, fan belt. We must all give absolutely everything.

 **Wenger Knows Best** @wengerknowsbest — May 17
Petrol, check. Handbrake, check. Brake pads, check. Fan belt, check. Fan belt well lubricated before kick-off, check.

 **Wenger Knows Best** @wengerknowsbest — May 17
Arsenal 3 Hull City 2 I'm still little bit magic! I wear a magic hat! And when I saw the FA Cup, I said I'm having that!

 **Wenger Knows Best** @wengerknowsbest — May 18
I must say, yesterday is little bit blur. I woke up smelling of champagne, with my shirt in pieces. Why? I don't know.

May 2014

Wenger Knows Best @wengerknowsbest   May 18
Overall, I believe our surprise plan to drop little bit physically in the first half lacked maybe little bit sharpness.

Wenger Knows Best @wengerknowsbest   May 18
Little bit silverware! Does anybody fancy little bit #OpenTopBusParade today? We are up for it.

Wenger Knows Best @wengerknowsbest   May 18
Am I still a 'specialist in failure'? Specialist, no. Is Mourinho now an 'apprentice in failure'? You have to ask him.

Wenger Knows Best @wengerknowsbest   May 18
We have lacked little bit sharpness and petrol this season, but the fan belt has shown exceptional consistency, with no handbrake niggle.

Wenger Knows Best @wengerknowsbest   May 18
I must say, the fan belt on today's parade showed outstanding gears, an exceptional engine and maybe little bit naughty language!

Wenger Knows Best @wengerknowsbest   May 18
I believe criticism of Wilshere's singing on today's parade is little bit harsh. I must say, I also think of Tottenham as a ship.

Wenger Knows Best @wengerknowsbest   May 18
Has this season been a success? I believe yes. It is not easy to win an FA Cup in a World Cup year, but we did it.

Wenger Knows Best @wengerknowsbest   May 19
"Morning Ivan. Yes, fantastic weekend! I know, we'll have to buy a '2014' for the stadium and move the other years. Little bit expensive."

May 2014

Wenger Knows Best @wengerknowsbest — May 19
When I said "Judge me in May", did I mean now? Yes, why not? Now seems an exceptionally good time.

Wenger Knows Best @wengerknowsbest — May 19
I believe Louis van Gaal is an outstanding appointment for Man Utd. Do we wish him well? Yes, although not too well.

Wenger Knows Best @wengerknowsbest — May 20
Are we leading the race for James Milner? I don't know. Is there a race? With fences? Little bit like Grand National? A race, no.

Wenger Knows Best @wengerknowsbest — May 20
Yaya Toure could not join us after his trial due to little bit work permit niggle. Don't worry, we didn't forget his birthday.

Wenger Knows Best @wengerknowsbest — May 20
I must tell you, all our players are wished happy birthday. We do not forget. Do they get the bumps too? No. But they might now.

Wenger Knows Best @wengerknowsbest — May 20
To avoid any little bit offence, I would like to wish a happy birthday to all our current players and any future ones. Congratulations!

Wenger Knows Best @wengerknowsbest — May 20
I can tell you, I am now close to exceptional news on my contract. How close? Look, close enough. Is there little bit surprise? Yes.

Wenger Knows Best @wengerknowsbest — May 20
I am delighted to announce that I have now signed my contract. For my book. 'Little Bit Silverware'. Congratulations!

May 2014

Wenger Knows Best @wengerknowsbest   May 20
Will 'Little Bit Silverware' be an outstanding book of
exceptional quality? I don't want to comment on publication.

Wenger Knows Best @wengerknowsbest   May 20
Is it a small relief for my book that we won the FA Cup? I
have been writing this book 30 years, I don't have to justify
every decision.

Wenger Knows Best @wengerknowsbest   May 20
Have I been writing my book 'Little Bit Silverware' since
February, with exceptional belief we would win the FA Cup?
Yes.

Wenger Knows Best @wengerknowsbest   May 20
Might Rio Ferdinand be little bit astute signing for this club?
Maybe yes. A Ferdinand is worth two in the bush.

Wenger Knows Best @wengerknowsbest   May 21
Are we swooping on Draxler? I can drive a stake through that,
it could be little bit fiction. I wouldn't count on Draxler.

Wenger Knows Best @wengerknowsbest   May 22
Have we thrown our hat into little bit ring for a shock move to
re-sign Ashley Cole? No. There is no hat and no ring.

Wenger Knows Best @wengerknowsbest   May 22
If there is a ring for re-signing Ashley Cole, will we throw our
hat into it? No. That could be dangerous. Little bit health
and safety.

Wenger Knows Best @wengerknowsbest   May 23
Is it possible for a talented young player not to be a
'wonderkid'? Are all wide players instantly 'wing wizards'? I
don't know.

May 2014

Wenger Knows Best @wengerknowsbest · May 23

Is Fabregas returning to this club? I can tell you, yes. He forgot to take his beard trimmer when he left. Little bit stubble niggle.

Wenger Knows Best @wengerknowsbest · May 23

"Ivan? Good evening...Yes I know, David Luiz ...very interesting. Okay, well errr let's bid £51......Pardon?...£50 MILLION!?!..."

Wenger Knows Best @wengerknowsbest · May 23

Have we released Bendtner? Yes, we wish him well. We thank him for errr... Well, for all his errr... Anyway, we wish him well.

Wenger Knows Best @wengerknowsbest · May 23

Have we released Ju Young Park? Sorry? Ju Young Park? No, no that name does not ring little bit bell. Park? Young? No.

Wenger Knows Best @wengerknowsbest · May 23

What will Bendtner do now? I don't know. Open little bit taxi business in Copenhagen? I don't know about that.

Wenger Knows Best @wengerknowsbest · May 23

Have I made a decision yet on dinner? No. But I am active in the market. If I find a dinner of exceptional quality, I will eat it.

Wenger Knows Best @wengerknowsbest · May 23

Have I eaten dinner yet? No. Am I close? Yes. How close? Look, I have been hungry 30 years, I don't have to justify every dinner.

Wenger Knows Best @wengerknowsbest · May 24

"Morning Ivan. Listen, has Bendtner actually left yet? No? Right. Call Chelsea. Tell them we'll take £40m..."

May 2014

Wenger Knows Best @wengerknowsbest · May 24
We congratulate QPR on winning promotion. I did not see the incident, but overall I believe it was a taxing afternoon for Redknapp.

Wenger Knows Best @wengerknowsbest · May 24
I feel little bit sorry for Steve McLaren, losing in the last minute is hard to take. But I don't like to comment on commiseration.

Wenger Knows Best @wengerknowsbest · May 24
Did Gareth Bale make the right decision to leave Tottenham for Real Madrid? Overall, I believe yes.

Wenger Knows Best @wengerknowsbest · May 25
Diego Simeone will be exceptionally low today. He did not see that coming. He expected Sergio Ramos to be sent off by then.

Wenger Knows Best @wengerknowsbest · May 25
We won the FA Cup, Real Madrid won the Champions League, Chelsea won nothing. Is Mourinho still 'The Happy One' today? I don't know.

Wenger Knows Best @wengerknowsbest · May 26
What is the latest on my contract? Well, I can tell you, the latest is that there is no latest. Thank you for your interest in my affairs.

Wenger Knows Best @wengerknowsbest · May 26
Are we close to little bit announcement on my contract? Look, I told you, I gave the club my word. Which word? I'm still not telling you.

Wenger Knows Best @wengerknowsbest · May 26
25 years ago tonight this club won a championship of exceptional ambition and outstanding quality, with absolutely no handbrake niggle.

May 2014

Wenger Knows Best @wengerknowsbest — May 26
Would it have been little bit poetic justice if we had beaten Liverpool 1-0? I don't want to comment on scant consolation.

Wenger Knows Best @wengerknowsbest — May 27
I feel this season we lacked maybe little bit offensive potential. Next season, potentially, we hope just to be offensive.

Wenger Knows Best @wengerknowsbest — May 27
Will Pochettino take over at Tottenham? I don't know, but now I have new lyrics to little bit Chi-lites classic 'Have you seen her?'

Wenger Knows Best @wengerknowsbest — May 27
"Oh I hear his name everywhere I go, on Sky Sports News and the radio. Pochettino, Mauricio Pochettino…"

Wenger Knows Best @wengerknowsbest — May 27
We wish Pochettino well at Tottenham. Will he last five years? We wish him well.

Wenger Knows Best @wengerknowsbest — May 27
Can Pochettino do well at Tottenham? I don't know. But if he is sacked on a 5-year deal, I believe he'll be Pochettino fortune.

Wenger Knows Best @wengerknowsbest — May 28
Well, I must say, we congratulate Pochettino on successfully completing one day as Tottenham manager. Is it a power shift? No.

Wenger Knows Best @wengerknowsbest — May 28
Do Tottenham still try to sign our transfer targets? I don't know. But, I must say, Danny Graham has exceptional quality.

May 2014

Wenger Knows Best @wengerknowsbest   May 29
Fabianski is close to joining Swansea. How close? Look, close. Will there be a welcome for him in the hillside? Yes, of course.

Wenger Knows Best @wengerknowsbest   May 29
I believe we have to accept that Sagna will leave this club. Did he give his word? Yes. What was it? Frankly, "non."

Wenger Knows Best @wengerknowsbest   May 29
Is Vermaelen going to Man Utd? I must tell you, yes. But the fixtures are not out for a few weeks, so I don't know when.

Wenger Knows Best @wengerknowsbest   May 30
Have I agreed a new contract with this club? Yes. Have I signed it yet? I'm not telling you.

Wenger Knows Best @wengerknowsbest   May 31
Now that we have won little bit silverware, will we open the war chest? Well, we are still not at war. And there is no chest.

Wenger Knows Best @wengerknowsbest   May 31
Have I agreed on terms with Loic Remy? Well, I can tell you, yes. I have agreed that 'Terms of Endearment' is little bit overrated.

Wenger Knows Best @wengerknowsbest   May 31
Have we expressed an interest in Cesc Fabregas? No. Do I know Fabregas? Yes. Do I need to express an interest? No.

Wenger Knows Best @wengerknowsbest   May 31
Now I have signed my contract I can assure you we will be super active in the market, to add top top quality in June, by July, late August.

We are absolutely delighted to land little
bit silverware.

Apparently it had been nine years since our last
trophy. I didn't know that, you would have thought
somebody would have mentioned it.

Am I still a specialist in failure? I believe no. I feel
I am once again, at the very least, an apprentice
in success.

I have three more years now at this club. I accept I
might not always know best, but I believe I do still
know something.

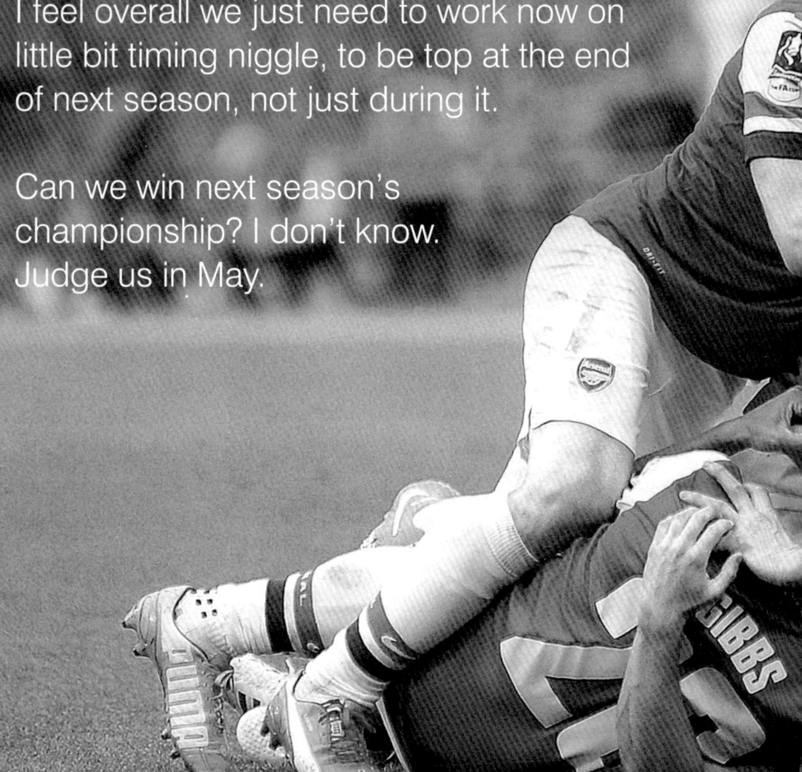
We congratulate Man City on winning
the championship.

We were top for 128 days this season, but we
accept they had outstanding miles to the gallon
and exceptional fuel efficiency.

But our FA Cup win shows that my players have
outstanding spirit, fantastic mental strength and
super potential. And thankfully Hull City dropped
little bit physically in the second half.

I feel overall we just need to work now on
little bit timing niggle, to be top at the end
of next season, not just during it.

Can we win next season's
championship? I don't know.
Judge us in May.

Well, I must say, this is the end of my book.

Did it have outstanding quality? I don't know,
I don't want to comment on publication.

I believe it showed exceptional potential. If I
can add one or two pages of top top quality
for next season's book, I will do it.

Overall, thank you for your interest in my affairs.

Acknowledgements

Well errr, this is little bit un-com-fort-able! I must tell you, I decided to maintain anonymity as I wish @wengerknowsbest and this book to stand on its merits, as a comic interpretation of Arsène Wenger and Wengerisms, not on the vanity of whoever I am. Overall, I didn't want to comment on speculation.

Footballistically, I must thank Arsène Wenger and Twitter. If it wasn't for them existing, this would be a blank page and there would be no book. I have always been good at impressions and have long recognised and mimicked Wenger's verbal traits and phraseology. I started @wengerknowsbest in April 2011 simply as I had a handful of Wengerish tweets that needed a comedy outlet. Partly intended to amuse myself, @wengerknowsbest has since gained a life and comic licence of its own. I never contemplated it would attract even 20 followers: three years and 5,000 tweets later, @wengerknowsbest has over 115,000 followers worldwide. I thank every one of them. It never purports to be Wenger, just to give an amusing Wengerish take, always meant in respect, never rude, never crude. If Arsène knows about it I hope he finds it amusing. At the very least, I hope he doesn't mind.

Huge literary thanks go to John Cross of the *Daily Mirror* and Jeremy Yates-Round of Haynes Publishing. John openly championed @wengerknowsbest and his easy rapport and enormous support helped to carve openings for me to write Daily Mirror articles and to meet Jeremy, a publisher, Arsenal fan and enthusiastic follower, to channel my book vision. Many thanks too to Amy Lawrence, of The Guardian and Observer.

Big credit goes to Simon Flavin and David Scripps at MirrorPix, for meticulously carving out suitable Wengerish images to meet my needs. Much gratitude to Kevin Gardner of BrainWave, for interpreting my photo spread mock-ups and colour coding for the mood photos.

A firm handshake goes to my editor Richard Havers, to copy editor Elizabeth Stone and proof-reader Rebecca Ellis, to Anthony Cooper at CampoRetro, Rob Burnett at the *Daily Mirror,* Paul Campbell at Piebury Corner and Arsenal's Mark Gonnella.. A manly hug goes to my good friend Alex Thomas for igniting my Twitter flame, his technical help with wengerknowsbest.com and for bellowing "Yeah! Get in!" when I won Best Comedy Football Blog at the 2013 Football Blogging Awards.

Crucially, I thank my beautiful wife and gorgeous kids. Words do not suffice. I dedicate this book to my late Dad and family and friends who aren't here to see this, but who would love it. While my identity is hardly national security, many thanks to close family and friends who do know and a "How about that!" to the others for when the façade drops. Here's to "Little Bit More Silverware" next season!